D1478823

INTERPRETING INTERNATIONAL POLITICS

Interpretive approaches to the study of international relations span not only the traditional areas of security, international political economy, and international law and organizations, but also emerging and newer areas such as gender, race, religion, secularism, and continuing issues of globalization. But how are we to bring interpretivist methods and concerns to bear on these topics? Cecelia Lynch focuses on the philosophy of science and conceptual issues that make work in international relations distinctly interpretive. This work both legitimizes and demonstrates the necessity of post- and non-positivist scholarship.

Lynch addresses each of the major, "traditional" subfields in International Relations, including International Law and Organization, International Security, and International Political Economy. By situating, describing, and analyzing major interpretive works in each of these fields, the book draws out the critical research challenges that are posed by and the progress that is made by interpretive work. Furthermore, the book also pushes forward interpretive insights to areas that have entered the IR radar screen more recently, including race and religion, demonstrating how work in these areas can inform all subfields of the discipline and suggesting paths for future research.

Cecelia Lynch is a professor in the department of political science at the University of California, Irvine. She is one of the original members of the "Methods Cafes" at the American Political Science Association, a forum for discussing interpretive methodologies. She has lectured at the Institute for Qualitative and Multi-Method Research (IQMMR) and at the Interpretive Methods workshop formed as part of the Northeastern Political Science Association, and acted as a faculty mentor at the NSF-funded Interpretive Methods and Methodologies workshop.

Routledge Series on Interpretive Methods
Edited by:
Dvora Yanow, University of Amsterdam
Peregrine Schwartz-Shea, University of Utah

The *Routledge Series on Interpretive Methods* comprises a collection of slim volumes, each devoted to different issues in interpretive methodology and its associated methods. The topics covered establish the methodological grounding for interpretive approaches in ways that distinguish interpretive methods from quantitative and qualitative methods in the positivist tradition. The series as a whole engages three types of concerns: 1) *methodological issues*, looking at key concepts and processes; 2) *approaches and methods*, looking at how interpretive methodologies are manifested in different forms of research; and 3) *disciplinary and subfield areas*, demonstrating how interpretive methods figure in different fields across the social sciences.

Interpretive Research Design: Concepts and Processes
Peregrine Schwartz-Shea and Dvora Yanow

Interpreting International Politics
Cecelia Lynch

Forthcoming:

Analyzing Social Narratives
Shaul R. Shenhav

Ethnography and Interpretation
Timothy Pachirat

Elucidating Social Science Concepts: An Interpretivist Guide
Frederic Charles Schaffer

Interviewing in Social Science Research: An Interpretive Approach
Lee Ann Fujii

International Advisory Board

Michael Agar
*Emeritus, University of Maryland
College Park, and Ethknoworks LLC,
Santa Fe, NM*

Mark Bevir
University of California, Berkeley

Pamela Brandwein
University of Michigan

Kevin Bruyneel
Babson College

Douglas C. Dow
University of Texas, Dallas

Vincent Dubois
University of Strasbourg

Raymond Duvall
University of Minnesota

Martha S. Feldman
University of California, Irvine

Lene Hansen
University of Copenhagen

Victoria Hattam
The New School

Emily Hauptmann
Western Michigan University

Markus Haverland
Erasmus University, Rotterdam

David Howarth
University of Essex

Patrick Thaddeus Jackson
American University

Timothy Kaufman-Osborn
Whitman College

Bernhard Kittel
Oldenburg University

Friedrich Kratochwil
European University Institute

Jan Kubik
Rutgers University

Beate Littig
Institute for Advanced Studies, Vienna

Joseph Lowndes
University of Oregon

Timothy Luke
Virginia Tech

Cecelia Lynch
University of California, Irvine

Navdeep Mathur,
India Institute of Management

Julie Novkov
State University of New York at Albany

Ido Oren
University of Florida

Ellen Pader
University of Massachusetts, Amherst

Kamal Sadiq
University of California, Irvine

Frederic C. Schaffer
University of Massachusetts, Amherst

Edward Schatz
University of Toronto

Ronald Schmidt, Sr.
California State University, Long Beach

James C. Scott
Yale University

Samer Shehata
Georgetown University

Diane Singerman
American University

Joe B. Soss
University of Wisconsin, Madison

Camilla Stivers
Cleveland State University

John Van Maanen
Massachusetts Institute of Technology

Katherine Cramer Walsh
University of Wisconsin, Madison

Lisa Wedeen
University of Chicago

Jutta E. Weldes
Bristol University

INTERPRETING INTERNATIONAL POLITICS

Cecelia Lynch

Routledge
Taylor & Francis Group

NEW YORK AND LONDON

First published 2014
by Routledge
711 Third Avenue, New York, NY 10017

and by Routledge
2 Park Square, Milton Park, Abingdon, Oxon OX14 4RN

Routledge is an imprint of the Taylor & Francis Group, an informa business

© 2014 Taylor & Francis

The right of Cecelia Lynch to be identified as author of this work
has been asserted by her in accordance with sections 77 and 78 of the
Copyright, Designs and Patents Act 1988.

All rights reserved. No part of this book may be reprinted or reproduced
or utilized in any form or by any electronic, mechanical, or other means,
now known or hereafter invented, including photocopying and recording,
or in any information storage or retrieval system, without permission in
writing from the publishers.

Trademark notice: Product or corporate names may be trademarks or
registered trademarks, and are used only for identification and explanation
without intent to infringe.

Library of Congress Cataloging-in-Publication Data
Lynch, Cecelia.
  Interpreting international politics / by Cecelia Lynch.
    pages cm. — (Routledge series on interpretive methods)
  1. International relations.   2. World politics.   I. Title.
  JZ1305.L95 2013
  327—dc23
  2013026425

ISBN: 978-0-415-89690-0 (hbk)
ISBN: 978-0-415-89691-7 (pbk)
ISBN: 978-0-203-80108-6 (ebk)

Typeset in Bembo
by Apex CoVantage, LLC

Printed and bound in the United States of America by Publishers Graphics,
LLC on sustainably sourced paper.

CONTENTS

SERIES EDITORS' FOREWORD

How might international politics be studied in an interpretive fashion? What makes such work, including the analyses undertaken by international relations (IR) scholars, distinctly interpretive? The first volume in the *disciplinary and sub-field areas* stream of the Routledge Series in Interpretive Methods, Cecelia Lynch's overarching view of IR scholarship provides those new to the discipline with a guide or map to negotiate a complex literature, while simultaneously challenging more seasoned IR researchers to understand their subfields in new ways.

Studies of international politics and international relations are key sites for understanding the power/knowledge nexus, an important focus for critical interpretive work. Reflection on the researcher's own role in the knowledge making enterprise is increasingly central to interpretive approaches to IR (as in other fields of inquiry), especially among feminist, critical theoretical, Gramscian, and post-colonial scholars. Whether it is traditional scholars' historical exclusions of various types of actors from conceptualizations of "security," Eurocentric legal assumptions about "human rights," or neoliberal prescriptions for the international political economy, the failure to theorize the place of scholars themselves in the structures of power is consistently challenged by interpretive scholarship. Lynch shows that interpretive presuppositions concerning what a researcher brings to her study (known as positionality), the intertwining of facts/values or power/ethics in that analysis, and the significance of context (historical, geographic, cultural) produce scholarship that questions conventional narratives of what matters in international politics and how what matters can and should be studied.

Lynch argues that interpretive approaches have been in play since the early years of IR research, and they can be found across its traditional subfields: security studies, international political economy, and international organization and law. She begins her analysis of the international politics literature by examining the interpretive underpinnings of much of the classical realist thought that dominated IR prior to the emergence and paradigmatic claims of neorealism. Then, beginning in the late 1980s, feminist scholars, among others, introduced a critical perspective that demonstrated the constructed character of security studies discourses, notably their seemingly "natural" neglect of women in analyses of the national interest. Interpretive work in international political economy has challenged that field's liberal and neoliberal narratives of progress, attending to the agency and resistance of those who least benefit from political and economic inequalities. And in international law and organizational studies, interpretive scholars have demonstrated the force of "words," belying neorealist claims of their irrelevance.

In concluding, Lynch challenges subfield boundaries and conceptualizations in examining interpretive work on race, religion, and the history of IR. She urges scholars to examine their own place in the power/knowledge nexus that in the past rendered race and religion, along with gender, irrelevant to scholarship. For Lynch, an *international* politics, a study of international relations *for* the world, means rejecting conventional understandings and histories. It requires, instead, a deep interrogation of commonplace verities promoted by the discourses of Western powers and a continual reflexivity by those who would endeavor to understand the possibilities for changing hitherto accepted policies, practices, and organizational arrangements.

Dvora Yanow, Wageningen University
Peregrine Schwartz-Shea, University of Utah

ACKNOWLEDGEMENTS

A book such as this one is both highly personal and highly dependent on the collective wisdom of intersecting groups of friends, scholars, and students. I have benefited enormously from the reading, engagement, and thoughtful responses of Dvora Yanow, Peregrine Schwartz-Shea, Catia Confortini, Nicholas Onuf, Xymena Kurowska, Tanya Schwarz, Steven Cauchon, and Carrie Reiling, as well as two anonymous readers. I thank each of them for their detailed comments and very welcome help, and all of my graduate students and interpretivist colleagues and friends for their engagement with the ideas and purpose of the book. I also thank Darcy Bullock and Michael Kerns at Routledge for their patience, which luckily for me, extended "all the way down" in the best interpretivist fashion. I dedicate this book to the memory of my aunt Charlyon, who, throughout my childhood in Independence, Missouri, always encouraged me to go out and experience the world.

Cecelia Lynch
Long Beach, California
July 2013

INTRODUCTION

Interpreting International Politics began with three objectives:

1) To zero in on the philosophy of science issues and concepts that make scholarship in international politics/international relations distinctly *interpretive*—
   oriented to discovering the many possible meanings of human experience in
   the world (as opposed to scholarship that assumes we can discover, through
   cumulative knowledge-generation, accurate representations of cause and
   effect in the world that all can agree on)—and demonstrate the reasons why
   interpretive IR is both necessary and legitimate in social science terms;
2) To address each of the major, "traditional," subfields in international relations,
   including international law and organization, international security, and international political economy, situating, describing, and analyzing the trajectory
   of major interpretive works in each of these fields to draw out critical research
   challenges posed and progress in the field made by interpretive work; and
3) To push forward interpretive insights to areas that have entered the IR radar
   screen more recently, especially regarding race, religion, and the genealogies
   of non-Western political histories, demonstrating how work in these areas
   can inform all subfields of the discipline and suggest paths for future research.

   In writing the book, however, I have come to realize that perhaps the most
important objective in addition to the three above is to show graduate students
and faculty how and why the body of interpretive work in international relations
demonstrates an impressive achievement.[1] There is now, in other words, a corpus
of interpretivist work that is notable and exciting in its reach across the subfields of IR, depth of conceptual and empirical understanding, and path-breaking

nature. This corpus of work has longstanding roots in the discipline. It is growing in volume and expanding in new directions, making new connections and developing new synergies. Interpretivisits, therefore, should take heart.

To clarify the core term, I employ "interpretive" as an adjective to modify forms of research, ontology, epistemology, and method and methodology that are centrally concerned with meaning; "interpretivist" as either a noun to describe those who conduct interpretive research or an adjective to denote descriptors by intentional scholarly actors (e.g. "interpretivist agendas"); and "interpretation" as the activity engaged in by interpretivist scholars. *Interpreting International Politics* demonstrates the breadth and depth of interpretivist work in IR, engaging with substantive/empirical and theoretical/conceptual issues that are foundational (if such a term can be used) for interpretive work. It does not provide a toolkit for how to do interpretive work or a comprehensive literature review of the corpus of material available. Rather, it examines significant interpretive concerns—both substantive and conceptual—that are strongly represented in international relations, how many of them are fruitfully addressed across a broad (although necessarily incomplete) selection of scholarship in traditional and emerging subfields, and how they can be promoted in future research to address gaps and provide new momentum on topics such as globalization, gender, alternative histories and forms of power, and ethical agency.

Here it is necessary to clarify what I mean by interpretivist work, and what criteria I have used to include some kinds of work that others might exclude, or exclude some kinds of work that others might include. As stated on p. 3, interpretivism focuses on the meaning of human experience—the variations in possible meanings for given events, how meaning is made through knowledge construction, how power and ethics constitute meaning, the implications of meaning for political and social phenomena. In Chapter 1, I identify six criteria that engage with questions about meaning which can mark scholarship as interpretivist. Not all of the examples I employ in the book reflect each of these criteria, at least not in equal measure. The differences in the use of interpretive criteria, I assert, are a necessary product of the nature of the interpretive enterprise in general, which is fluid in definition rather than rigidly bounded, but these differences also reflect the particular character of interpretation in the field of IR. As a result, my interpretation of what qualifies will differ from those of others, as there is no Archimedean point from which to judge research as one type or another—it really is interpretation all the way down.[2] Nevertheless, my logic should be sufficiently transparent for others to form their own judgments, and there should be significant overlaps between my categorizations of interpretivist scholarship and those of other interpretivists in the field. As a result, I argue in favor of a legacy of interpretation in IR that is strong, enduring, ongoing, and even expanding, but still fluid.

I define this legacy on substantive as well as conceptual grounds. Central to it, for example, is the work of early IR theorists, who were concerned with the relationship between power and morality and debated how to interpret the actions and statements of government officials and how to understand the implications of immediate actions given longer-term processes and practices. In other words, they were concerned with what has become known as the "agent-structure problem" (Wendt 1987), and viewed power as slippery and contingent rather than determined by covering laws or material structures alone. Equally central is the role of feminist and critical international relations in blazing interpretive paths, both in bringing central interpretive insights into IR theory *writ large* and in making crucial, ongoing interventions into debates about methodology and method. Feminist theorists have brought to the forefront substantive demonstrations of the partiality and power relations of knowledge construction, and the completely different interpretations that can result from denaturalizing international politics according to the insights of feminist theorizing.

IIP also engages with critical, linguistic, and pragmatic forms of constructivism, as well as other forms of critical and postpositivist work. The book does not address constructivism that self-identifies as either "positivist" or "modernist," not because interpretation is absent in such work, but instead because it consciously rejects many of the orientations and insights (for example, the symbiotic nature of "fact" and "value") that I assert in Chapter 1 are critical to the interpretive enterprise. Other forms of theorizing are less self-conscious about distancing themselves from interpretivist assumptions. For example, some characteristics of Gramscian and critical feminist scholarship could be categorized as non-interpretivist. However, I include them in Chapter 3 on International Political Economy. What I find interpretive about much Gramscian work in IR is its fascinating and, I think, apt connection between cultural and material hegemony and the "consent" of the governed in the production of hegemonic rule. Such consent may be implicit, explicit, or both, but the production and reproduction of consent require a constitutive approach to concepts such as rationality, intentionality, power and knowledge. And, while some Gramscians might argue that their understandings of the world represent a type of "objective" reality, the very idea that power and knowledge are used for particular purposes requires interpretation—uncovering the forms of power as well as their meanings and implications for specific political processes. Similarly, one could quibble with my inclusion of critical constructivism, which frequently tends towards structuralist and neo-Gramscian analyses of power, even while it claims Foucault as a primary influence. Constructivism in IR has been "disciplined" into positivist and interpretivist sectors (Klotz and Lynch 2007), which, in addition to other problems, can obfuscate the insights provided by interpretivist social theory and methodologies. As a result, constructivism in IR has become a grab-bag for non-structuralist and non-rational choice work of many kinds, which has its virtues in opening the space for a wide variety of work to be done, but which also has its drawbacks in moving attention away from the relationship between constructivism's social construction*ist* antecedents (in the work of Anthony Giddens, for example) and other precursors in philosophy and social theory (for example, Ludwig Wittgenstein and Michel Foucault).[3] As a result, the critical nature of the interpretive enterprise in IR—uncovering and exposing alternative interpretations of power—has guided my selection and inclusion of this scholarship.

This volume, therefore, addresses the interplay of conceptual and substantive issues at stake in interpretive work by highlighting feminist, constructivist, and other postpositivist research in IR that follows the interpretivist premises outlined in the next chapter. In IR, the terms postpositivist and poststructural are closely related, although they refer to somewhat different things. "Poststructuralism" in IR has very particular meanings, because of the hold that structural forms of theorizing (especially realism and Marxism) had on the field as the Cold War developed. The end of the Cold War, conversely, posed serious challenges to structuralist premises, not least because they had no means of explicating the revolutionary events that it comprised. Postpositivism, however, refers to a range of epistemological approaches that reject inductively based, nomological causal analyses (see Kratochwil 1989; Jackson 2011; Schwartz-Shea and Yanow 2012). Interpretivism is inevitably postpositivist in my view (see Chapter 1). But it is not the only type of postpositivism: both critical rationalism and the "scientific" realism that Alexander Wendt draws on also move away from inductive positivism to at least quasi-deductive reasoning, although still with the assumption that scholars can discover "covering laws" to explain the world in more-or-less ahistorical terms.

Both poststructuralism and postpositivism are critical to the types of scholarship examined in this book. While interpretivists are content for the most part to claim postpositivist philosophical grounding, the move away from structuralisms, especially given the post-Cold War context, is a necessity for interpretivists in IR. Yet some make this move more cleanly than others. Thus a range of positions vis-à-vis practices and institutions such as the balance of power, or economic hegemony, are not only possible in interpretivist work but are readily seen in the rest of this book.

Regarding the pages that follow, there are a number of ways in which one could write a book about interpretation in international politics. For example, one could focus on research in IR that employs specific methodologies such as discourse analysis, narrative, ethnography, participant observation, in-depth interviews, or interpretive archival analysis. Or one could emphasize the metatheoretical and even metaphysical philosophical trajectory underlying interpretivism in IR, focusing on how interpretivist IR scholars draw heavily on theorists such as Aristotle, Hobbes, Hume, Kant, Weber, Wittgenstein, Heidegger, Gramsci, Gadamer, Foucault, Haraway, Derrida, Lacan, Kristeva, Bourdieu, and numerous others (see Chapter 1). Either of these would represent a strong addition to the interpretivist canon, although elements of the first have already been done (despite the fact that more literature to be plumbed is constantly being added), and the second also has several excellent, existing versions (e.g. Edkins and Vaughan-Williams 2009).

I have instead chosen to write a book organized by conventional IR subfields that emphasizes the relationship among substantive, conceptual, and ethical concerns in the field. I have done so for personal or idiosyncratic reasons as well as political ones. My own work is motivated by an ongoing engagement and passion with the implications of this relationship, so this is the book I am best positioned to write. I address the political concerns more fully in the concluding chapter, but suffice it to say here that, for me, recognizing that interpretive scholarship has shaped, at least in part, each of the discipline's subfields is an exercise in demonstrating its endurance and power. Students can perhaps, as a result, see their own concerns as part of a broader trajectory or series of trajectories. Interpretivists can perhaps take on a less defensive posture vis-à-vis others in epistemological and methodological debates. Journal editors might be able to see that IR scholarship is indeed quite broad, and policy-makers can possibly draw more easily on work that demonstrates ethical dilemmas rather than assuming that linear progress, without critique, is possible or even desirable.

This book, therefore, is intended for international relations scholars, including faculty and graduate students in all IR subfields (including traditional subfields of security, political economy, law and organization), and also feminists and the increasing number of scholars and students who cross the lines of political theory and international relations or participate in newly emerging subfields of race and religion. It can also be useful in upper-level undergraduate courses in international relations and related subjects, and others outside of IR, including policy-makers, might even decide to peruse it. More importantly, it is intended to provide legitimation for IR scholars and students to conduct and publish research that forces us—scholars, students, policy-makers, the public—to challenge received assumptions about how the world works.

Positioning this Book vis-à-vis Methodological Interventions in IR

This book is about interpretivist substance and concepts and their methodological implications for the field of IR, but it does not demarcate the boundaries of specific methodological choices (such as discourse analysis, ethnography, etc.). Some scholars have done that already; still others are engaged in specifying the bases and mechanisms of given interpretive methodologies in other volumes in this series. The first trajectory began with a path-breaking 1999 article by Jennifer Milliken, "The Study of Discourse in International Relations: A Critique of Research and Methods," published in the *European Journal of International Relations,* and since Milliken's intervention interpretive international relations scholars have debated the value of making methodological concerns explicit in their work.[4] Milliken emphasized in particular the methodological implications for IR of the "linguistic turn" (the insight that language cannot accurately represent an objectively determined reality, but can only reflect socially mediated understandings). While important voices such as that of Raymond Duvall have argued against an over-reliance on "method-ism," others have asserted that articulating the approaches, ontological assumptions, forms of research methods, and standards of validity in the field are critical. This volume acknowledges and appreciates Duvall's worry that "method-ism," if taken too far, can foster the idea that there is an appropriate, cookie-cutter method for each international relations problem, and that technique and application then become the primary concerns for the researcher. Nevertheless, the articulation, discussion, and debate of "methodologies" (or the intellectual processes that guide research, as defined by Ackerly, Stern, and True 2006), as part of a broader discussion of their conceptual underpinnings, is crucial for interpretive international relations for at least two reasons: 1) to assist interested scholars whose mentors do not employ interpretive work, which also entails making interpretive work understandable for behavioralist-oriented colleagues, and 2) to increase and deepen productive dialogue among interpretivists in order to enhance scholarship, creativity, and new insights. Indeed, Duvall himself, along with other scholars, has advanced this type of attention to concept and methodology in his own publications (for example, on Edward Said's "contrapuntal methodology" articulated in Duvall and Varadarajan 2007, discussed in Chapter 5; and on critical constructivism in Weldes, Laffey, Gusterson, and Duvall 2000). As a result, there is good reason to expose and highlight the intersections among methodology, concepts, and substantive interventions by interpretivists in the field.

Since the publication of Milliken's article, a number of additional methodological interventions in international relations have appeared. These include the series of edited volumes on constructivism in IR published by M.E. Sharpe (*International Relations in a Constructed World,* edited by Kubálková, Onuf, and Kowert 1998, *Foreign Policy in a Constructed World,* edited by Kubálková 2001, and *Constructing International Relations: The Next Generation,* edited by Fierke and Jørgensen 2001), the volume co-authored by Klotz and Lynch in the same series (*Strategies for Research in Constructivist International Relations,* 2007), edited volumes on feminist methodology (Ackerly, Stern, and True, *Feminist Methodologies for International Relations,* 2006; and Ackerly and True, *Doing Feminist Research in Political and Social Science,* 2010), a book on discourse analysis (Hansen, *Security as Practice: Discourse Analysis and the Bosnian War,* 2006), and a co-edited Palgrave Macmillan volume on selected research methods (Klotz and Prakash, *Qualitative Methods in International Relations: A Pluralist Guide,* 2009). General volumes on methodological debates in the field of political science, including those edited by Dvora Yanow and Peregrine Schwartz-Shea (*Interpretation and Method: Empirical Research Methods and the Interpretive Turn,* 2006/2103) and Kristin Renwick Monroe (*Perestroika!* 2005), include chapters by international relations scholars but are not focused on IR *per se.* Finally, there now exist several introductory international relations textbooks on the undergraduate level that privilege interpretive research agendas and ethical concerns. These include volumes by Maja Zehfuss and Jenny Edkins, eds (2009), Steven Lamy, John Baylis, Patricia Owen, and Steve Smith (2011),

Laura Shepherd (2010), and Cynthia Weber (2005). Each of these texts demonstrates that it is possible to present critical and interpretive international relations concepts to entry-level undergraduate students through the study of particular international issue-areas, film, or other innovative means.

Each of these books represents exciting interventions in the field of political science and/or the subfield of international relations. This volume, however, differs from each of them in important ways. The most obvious difference is in its subject matter and organization: the subject matter includes only interpretivist work in IR (as I have defined it in the following chapter), but it strives to span the broad range of post-positivist assumptions, contributions, debates, and new thinking that this work represents. It does not emphasize meta-theoretical issues, but it does focus on conceptual underpinnings and their relationship to substantive events, and it delineates several significant findings in philosophy of science literatures on social phenomena that are of special importance to international relations scholars. Finally, in emphasizing the intersection of methodological and substantive issues that arises for international relations scholarship, it is unique in addressing the stakes and status of interpretive approaches for each of the major subfields of IR: security, international political economy, and law and organization, as well as new and cross-cutting topics and fields of religion and race. Although the status of interpretive work can only be captured loosely because research continues to proliferate in many directions, a number of specific themes and questions that are examined by this book continue to connect past, present, and very likely future interpretive work. This book provides an opportunity, therefore, to assess where interpretive work in IR has come and where it is going in the twenty-first century.

Outline of the Book

The next chapter engages in more detail the premises, goals and processes involved in interpretive scholarship. Following this, subsequent chapters, on international security, international political economy, international law and organization, race, religion, and histories and futures in IR, display several common themes. Most significant is that they challenge the knowledge constructed and reproduced as "fact" by scholars and policy-makers alike. This knowledge is most often packaged as "systemic" or structural in some sense. It includes "systems" of international anarchy, balance of power, the liberal global economy, and international law. It also includes assumptions based on male and masculinized experience and, as the last chapter in particular demonstrates, representations of naturalized racial (white, of European origin) and religious (Christian, or Enlightenment secular) identities and ethics.

Each chapter addresses interpretive work in its particular subfield, beginning with more historical work in order to reflect the endurance and importance of interpretivism in that subfield, and ending with newer work and/or work that does not fit easily into the chronology of subfield genres. The chronologies are of necessity loose, however, because they are meant to address significant themes that have arisen at particular historical junctures, rather than provide a comprehensive history from decade to decade. Some historical junctures, such as the end of the Cold War, prompted multiple genres of new work within and/or across sub-disciplines, reflecting the interplay between "theory" and "praxis." Chapters are also organized, therefore, according to both conceptual and substantive themes, providing an opportunity to assess the mutual constitution of knowledge with world events over the course of the history of the discipline.

Notes

1 I call the book "Interpreting International *Politics*", yet I consistently refer to inter-pretive work in international *relations*. This is because I want to focus on the more expansive nature of the political in what we actually try to figure out in our scholar-ship, but the field itself has a slightly different name, which focuses attention on states and their interrelationships as the foundational subject of study. The field has been referred to as "IR" for well over a century.
2 I learned of the absence of Archimedean points from Fritz Kratochwil, and will always be indebted to him for it.
3 It is an open question whether this disciplining also impoverishes both positivist-leaning and post-positivist constructivist scholarship.
4 As this book hopes to make clear, interpretive work itself in IR began much earlier than 1999, and has existed since the beginnings of the discipline in the early twentieth century.

1

INTERPRETIVE CONCEPTS, GOALS, AND PROCESSES IN INTERNATIONAL RELATIONS

What kinds of research in IR are interpretive?
What are the primary concepts and goals guiding interpretive research in IR?
How is interpretivism in IR different from logical positivist or critical rationalist work?
How are responses to these questions incorporated into interpretivist research in the major subfields of IR?

Interpretive research is alive, well, and expanding in international relations, examining an increasing range of substantive, theoretical, and conceptual problems. Interpretivists, for example, challenge conventional understandings of international security for promoting militarized solutions to conflicts and creating gendered hierarchies of issues considered to be significant for international politics. They call into question the liberal assumptions of truisms regarding wealth generation and poverty relief, pointing out the voices and societies left out of these assumptions. They trace the genealogy of international legal norms and institutions to demonstrate their racialized nature in contexts of decolonization. They analyze the linguistic properties, rules and norms, discourse and power relations involved in the construction and maintenance of these and a host of other practices and processes in international relations. This chapter discusses the reasons for and bases of interpretive work in IR, focusing on its goals, its differences with non-interpretive research, and the substantive problems in world politics that have prompted its various forms to take hold. In addressing these issues, the chapter also explicates the major questions in philosophy of science and social theory that make interpretive research possible, necessary, and valid.

Interpretivism has a long history in IR, although one might be forgiven today for not recognizing it. IR as a discipline was founded in Progressive Era desires to professionalize social knowledge (late nineteenth–early twentieth century, see

Carr 1946), but these desires did not translate into ahistorical or nomothetic theorizing.[1] Instead, early debates about the international addressed the character, malleability, and durability of law in the international realm, as well as whether attempts to engineer progress were feasible or desirable. While classical realists criticized what they saw as the liberal biases of those they called utopians (or idealists), this first great debate in international relations (Lapid 1989) can also be seen as a struggle largely fought on interpretive grounds among a range of contested interpretations of power, security, morality, and law (Long and Wilson 1995; Long and Schmidt 2005; Ashworth 2008). Classical realists are frequently lauded for their skeptical worldview (Loriaux 1992; Shou Tjalve 2008), while their peace movement opponents are sometimes (mis)characterized as liberal positivists. I assert, however, that these opponents incorporated a fair share of skepticism as well as critical and even dystopic thinking into their debates about how to achieve a more just and peaceful global order (Lynch 1999).[2]

The development of nineteenth and early twentieth century social theory was also critical for interpretive work in international relations. Marx and Engels created the field of critical political economy, late nineteenth century theorists such as Wilhelm Dilthey articulated the bases of hermeneutics for the philosophy of science, early twentieth century social theorists, especially Max Weber, blazed new paths in understanding the forms of rationalization that were characteristic of modernity, and critical theorists in the Frankfurt School connected disciplinary to political forms of power and demonstrated the dangers of their normalization. Similarly, Antonio Gramsci incorporated culture and phenomenology into Marxist analysis through developing his concept of ideological and cultural hegemony, and Friedrich Nietzsche probably went the farthest in blasting open the boundaries of ethical debate through his unrelenting critique of moral foundationalism (Der Derian 1987; Gill 1993; Cox 1996). IR scholars would draw on these and many other thinkers throughout the twentieth and into the twenty-first centuries (for a more comprehensive treatment than there is space for here, see Edkins and Vaughan-Williams 2009, and Roach 2008).

Interpretivist scholarship continued to develop during and after the Second World War, including by British writers and diplomatic historians (E.H. Carr, Martin Wight and Herbert Butterfield, among others), political sociologists such as Raymond Aron in France, and across the Atlantic, Karl Polanyi and Albert Wolfers. Each of these scholars related political and economic phenomena to historical and cultural contexts in ways that placed the variability of meaning at the forefront of analysis. Polanyi assessed the constitutive nature of the development of market, state, and culture in his seminal work, *The Great Transformation* (1944), while Wolfers (as discussed in the next chapter), acknowledged the ambiguity of the "symbol" of national security in an influential *World Politics* journal article (Wolfers 1952).

Thus far most of the interpretive debates and insights I have pointed to were carried out by white men in Europe and North America. Yet, interpretive interventions that shape IR come from a larger group of thinkers and scholars and reflect a much broader geographic, racial, and gender diversity. Frantz Fanon's writings, especially *The Wretched of the Earth* (1961), influenced generations of postcolonial interpretivists in IR, and scholars are recovering the earlier impact of W.E.B. DuBois and Mohandas Gandhi on decolonization struggles and movements against racism, poverty, and other forms of marginalization (Muppidi 2009). Interpretive IR scholars are increasingly bringing to light the work of additional thinkers from across the globe (Grovogui 2006; Tickner 2008) who have challenged Western assumptions regarding the meanings of international phenomena and have articulated new insights regarding debates about sovereignty and human rights, as discussed in Chapters 4 and 5.

Nor has feminism been absent from the earliest debates in IR. Feminist writers from Virginia Woolf in the 1920s to Simone Weil in the 1930s to Simone de Beauvoir in the 1940s and Elise Boulding in the 1970s made critical interventions that informed IR scholarship directly or indirectly, by challenging assumptions underlying the gendered nature of war, peace, property rights, and ethics. Feminist postcolonial theorists more recently have altered the nature of gender debates in the field. Their insights demonstrate, for example, how the theories of the colonizers dismiss the voices and experiences of the "subaltern," challenging liberal feminist assumptions regarding what constitutes women's oppression and influencing much contemporary postpositivist work (Spivak 1988, 1998; Kinnvall 2009). Finally, feminist research on science and philosophy has expanded interpretive IR understandings of the gendered nature of knowledge production to incorporate the concept of "embodied knowledge" (Haraway 2003).

This somewhat eclectic genealogy shows that if international relations has forgotten to a large extent its interpretivist origins and history, contemporary students interested in interpretivism should return to it for inspiration and validation regarding their assumptions, concepts, and frameworks. Interpretivists in IR appeal to a wide range of philosophers and social theorists to provide the ontological and epistemological bases for their research questions. Nineteenth and twentieth century social theory and philosophy of science shape contemporary interpretivism, but many scholars trace their concerns to ancient and medieval as well as modern theorists. Bringing in ethics, virtue, and the political nature of humans takes us back to Aristotle and the Greeks as well as Cicero and the Romans, moving through early and medieval Christian, Jewish and Muslim thought (e.g. Augustine, Maimonides, Ibn Khaldun), to Kant, Nietzsche, and Arendt. Debates about cosmopolitanism, law and world government, and peace and conflict return us to Hobbes, Kant, Grotius, and Vitoria.[3] The focus on meaning, including the variability of appeals to science, steers us to Weber and feminist theorists such as Haraway. Interpretivists in IR cannot do without nineteenth and twentieth century theorists of the "linguistic turn," especially Dilthey and Wittgenstein, and the connection to language and power necessitates bringing in Nietzsche, Foucault and Derrida. Debates about agency and structure emphasize implicit or explicit notions of practice that stem from feminists as well as Giddens, Geertz, and

Bourdieu. Finally, decentering the West requires critical and postcolonial analyses that draw on insights from Marx but move on to Gramsci, Fanon, Spivak, and Said, among others (Edkins and Vaughan-Williams 2009).

These and other scholars, writers, public intellectuals, and activists have articulated concepts and developed ways of thinking that allow interpretivists in international relations to explore the meaning of relations of power, race, gender, and class, the process of constructing otherness, the difference between ideal-typical classification schemes and historical layering, and the possibilities and constraints of ethical intentionality and moral action. As a result, interpretive IR continues to expand into new territories, literal and figurative.

Concepts and Goals of Interpretive Research in International Relations

The historiography of IR demonstrates that it was largely founded and developed as an interpretivist discipline. In focusing on how meanings are made, interpretivists have challenged taken-for-granted assumptions and orthodoxies, raised new questions, and articulated new ways of examining "old" questions. They have made visible the workings of power that orthodoxies covered up, exposed the contradictions in conventional explanations of world politics, and brought new and marginalized voices into the analysis of power relations. They have pointed out the conceptual and empirical problems in pursing the goal of an elusive "synthesis," either in cosmopolitan or theoretical terms. They have addressed important questions of ethics, either implicitly or explicitly. Some have maintained that the role of research should also be emancipatory, while others have disclaimed such goals. In either case, most have insisted on reflexivity, i.e., the injunction continually to reassess and reflect on their positionality in international relations research (Alcoff 1988), including how their situated identities are related to their political (and scholarly) projects, because this positionality is part and parcel of the process and content of knowledge construction. This means they provide insight into the sociology, historiography, and ethics of the discipline, raising new conceptual and substantive questions in the process. These features lead to issues regarding philosophies of science, the role of discourse, and the workings of power.

Central Concepts in the Focus on Meaning

Turning to popular philosophers can be extremely useful for understanding the importance of meaning. In the Monty Python sketch, 'Spectrum'—talking about things, Michael Palin plays a news announcer who brings in "the Professor" (John Cleese) and a pundit (Graham Chapman) to talk about the meaning of things, or "that old vexed question of what is going on." To explain what is going on, the pundit excitedly shows a graph with columns representing "23 . . ., 28 . . ., and 43 percent of the population!!!" But he does not tell us what the graphs are referring to (23 percent of the United Kingdom's population own pigs? 43 percent of the world's population eat pasta, identify as transsexual, or have children under the age of five?), or whether he is excited by the simple existence or nonsense of the graphs. As a result, we have no referent or context to decide what the statistics might mean. As Michael Palin's announcer says, "Telling figures indeed, but what do they mean to you, what do they mean to me, what do they mean to the average man [sic] in the street?"

This sketch again underscores the need to analyze the *meaning* of phenomena and the variety of human experience (as stated in the Introduction), and to do so in *contexts* that are relevant for such meaning. As Peregrine Schwartz-Shea and Dvora Yanow argue in the initial volume of this series, the *sine qua non* of interpretive research is its emphasis on meaning-making, or "knowledge *about what?*" Interpretivism "seeks knowledge about how human beings, scholars included, make individual and collective sense of their particular worlds," resulting in, as Nicholas Onuf puts it, a "world of our making" (Schwartz-Shea and Yanow 2012: 46; Onuf 1989).

Interpretation is an integral part of seeking knowledge about meaning in ways that are sometimes masked by truisms in the IR field. For example, Oxford philosopher of science Mary Hesse highlights one of the central problems of social science research: events that scholars try to explain are underdetermined (Hesse 1978). This insight contrasts directly with assumptions that inform research on major turning points in international relations. In IR, events are frequently said to be overdetermined—that is, there appear to be an abundance of factors that are demonstrable "causes," and so the task (as non-interpretivists see it) becomes sorting through them systematically to find out which *one* is the *real* cause. International relations scholars' continued attempts to explain the First World War, for example, are frequently based on assumptions of overdetermination, given the influence of numerous factors at varying levels of analysis including the personality of Kaiser Wilhelm II, Serbian and German nationalism, British and French imperialism, military mobilizations in Central Europe, and the naval arms race between Britain and Germany (Joll 2000). Other instances of overdetermination might be the end of the Cold War, the causes of September 11, 2001, or going further back historically, the signing of the Peace of Westphalia and the development of the modern state system (Thomas 2005; Philpott 2000; Nexon 2009). Yet Hesse, following Quine, points out that phenomena are underdetermined by the available evidence. In other words, evidence can never prove without a doubt that a given social or political event emanates from a specific cause, which is why, for example, all of the above "causes" of the First World War continue to be debated. As a result, the attempt by conventional social science to view "overdetermination" as a problem, and multiple factors as in need of winnowing down to a single "necessary and sufficient" cause, is misplaced. For our purposes, this insight means that we cannot isolate a single, determinative cause for world-changing events like the end of the Thirty Years' War, the beginning of World War I, or the end of the Cold

War. The upshot of this problem—which cannot be completely overcome, despite the existence of differing degrees of underdetermination (Laudan 1990)—is that we always rely on interpretation to assign any type of causality to the relationship between the political phenomena we think exist and the political outcomes we think we observe. (We do this through abductive reasoning, as discussed later in this chapter.) Everyone interprets, although everyone does not consider herself to be an interpretivist! For our purposes, the problem of underdetermination, giving rise to the "interpretive gap" in assessing causality, also means that dominant explanations—shaped by the workings of power—generally take over, filling the spaces between events and our understandings of them and growing in influence with their continual reproduction. This is why thorough contextualization of political phenomena is important for interpretivists. One of the main objectives of much interpretive research in IR, as a result, is to denaturalize dominant explanations, exposing them not as truth but as narratives that are discursively constructed, assigned particular meanings, and reproduced from partial or limited evidence and with particular stakes or purposes in mind, and to provide evidence that indicates the possibility or plausibility of other articulations and meanings of the phenomena in question.

While all research of any epistemology relies on interpretation implicitly or explicitly, interpretivist scholarship also *challenges both the fact/value distinction and the correspondence theory of truth* (Taylor 1971/1977). Many who doubt the legitimacy of interpretivism incorrectly claim that postpositivists reject "facts."[4] Instead, scholars in interpretivist traditions strongly reject the claim that things, social facts, and events can be separated from the "value" attached to them by participants, observers, and evaluators. A glass of wine can abet the disease of alcoholism, the conviviality of a party, or the romantic attachment of a couple, depending on the prior experiences and current orientations of the observers and participants. More importantly, different groups of people *think* that a glass of wine can do one or several of these things, depending on how their experiences, contexts, and values shape the meanings they assign to it, and they react to, use, or reject it accordingly. The glass of wine can also represent something evil or sacred, depending on the traditions and meanings assigned by different religious and cultural communities. A nuclear warhead can be described by its shape, color, type of metal, and atomic contents, but it takes on values of protection, terror, masculinized violence, or a combination thereof depending on the interpretive community, which develops and assigns to it an "intersubjective" meaning—one that is taken as fact by its members. A World Bank-funded dam can be evaluated primarily by the amount of energy it generates or the number of homes and livelihoods its construction has destroyed. The value we place on each will shape our understanding of the "fact" of the dam and the expectations that we draw from its existence.

Non-interpretivist researchers generally prioritize the attempt to understand the essence of the phenomenon apart from any intersubjectively assigned value. Their goal, for example, is to understand the "objective" value, defined according to a specific metric, of the World Bank-funded dam. Interpretivists view this as an impossible task without taking into consideration the meanings that groups of people assign to the dam, because things and the values attached to them are inseparable. Interpretivists also see the symbiotic nature of "fact" and "value" as providing critical research questions in their own right. A simple example is that military arsenals cannot be assessed objectively as producing either safety or threat without understanding who possesses them, against whom they are targeted, and how the construction of those against whom they are targeted as "enemies" has taken place.

The symbiotic relationship between fact and value leads many interpretivists to argue that there is no such thing as an "objective" analysis in the social sciences. However, some feminists reorient this argument, asserting that "broadening the base from which knowledge is constructed, that is, including the experiences of women, can actually enhance objectivity" (Tickner 1997: 622). J. Ann Tickner points out that the work of both Sandra Harding and Donna Haraway makes claims in this regard. Harding, for example,

> explores the question as to whether objectivity and socially situated knowl-
> edge is an impossible combination. She concludes that adopting a feminist
> standpoint actually strengthens standards of objectivity. While it requires
> acknowledging that all human beliefs are socially situated, it also requires
> critical evaluation to determine which social situations tend to generate the
> most objective knowledge claims.
>
> *(Tickner 1997: 622)*

Harding's term for this is "strong objectivity," which, according to Tickner, "extends the task of scientific research to include a systematic examination of powerful background beliefs and making strange what has hitherto appeared as familiar" (Tickner 1997: 622). Donna Haraway makes a similar claim in articulating the concept of "embodied objectivity." This type of objectivity comes from "situated knowledge," which Tickner argues is intended to enable "'better accounts of the world' (Haraway 1988: 580)" (Tickner 1997: 622).

These debates lead to the insight that phenomena in IR (as in other fields) are referred to in multiple ways. The *type of language* used not only provides descriptors but also incorporates moral judgment. International law experts point out that such judgment sometimes requires legal action. For example, "circumcision" refers to genital cutting done for cultural, religious, or health reasons, but "female genital mutilation" refers to a ritual condemned by international norms, although variations of the practice are defended in numerous local communities. Even more to the point, if the UN Security Council uses the term "genocide" instead of "group or ethnic killing" to describe a conflict, the provisions of UN Charter Chapter VII are supposed to be put into motion because genocide requires action to stop it according to international law. If an NGO or an aggrieved population employs the term, however, international law is not necessarily mobilized, although using the term may signal the beginning of a discursive struggle over the meaning of the events. And if the Security Council employs a different term such as "civil war" to describe the same conflict, then the Council has much wider decision-making latitude before any decision to act is taken.

Such examples illustrate the linguistic properties at the heart of international "institutions," or sets of rule-determined practices (Onuf 2012). The "linguistic turn" in the philosophy of science challenged the correspondence theory of truth, or the idea that language could exactly reflect and represent reality. Ludwig Wittgenstein's later work was key in moving away from the correspondence theory to a more interpretive stance which asserted that all understandings of reality were socially (and hence linguistically) mediated (Wittgenstein 1953/1958; Fierke 1998). Moreover, Wittgenstein's later work demonstrated that understanding the rule-bound nature of "language games" could provide insight into the intersubjective setting, or space, in which social and political practices are carried out. The link between intersubjectivity, language, and institutions is constitutive, as Charles Taylor points out (Taylor 1977: 121). That is to say, intersubjective meanings, expressed through some forms of language (and not others), along with institutional practices, shape each other's existence and reproduction; there is no single-direction causal arrow between one and the other. As a result, "there is no extra-discursive realm from which material, objective facts assert themselves" (Hansen 2006: 33).

Another linguistic approach employed by some interpretivists in IR draws on the work of Ferdinand de Saussure, who, according to Peterson, argues that the relationship between "the signifier (word/symbol) and the signified (that for which it stands; the object or entity)" is "arbitrary." While the possibilities for choosing signifiers are theoretically endless, "the signifying process stabilizes or partially 'fixes' meaning/interpretation by codifying differences in particular ways" (Peterson 2003: 41). Language, then, is "a system of signification/codification, it enables us to impose a particular structure/ordering on our experience and to communicate that experience intersubjectively" (Peterson 2003: 42). This terminology represents another expression of the rejection of the fact/value distinction. Derrida, in articulating the concept of "difference," took this a step further to assert that things have no meaning or essence in themselves, but only in relation to other things— meaning lies in this difference, or opposition. Given a surplus of possible signifiers, then, meaning is constructed out of opposition to other signifiers. The resulting fixity or stabilization is never absolute, allowing the possibility of fluctuation and change. Nevertheless, the resulting "systems of intelligibility" are constructed "at the expense of alternative stabilizations/orderings" and shape "our subjectivities, our knowledge of the world, and our practices within it" (Peterson 2003: 42).

Interpretivists agree, then, that language can only approximate or reflect a part of reality rather than representing reality or truth in a total or holistic sense because language is socially mediated and temporally and geographically conditioned. As a result, interpretivists acknowledge the importance of the *hermeneutic circle*. The researcher herself is part and parcel of the socially mediated conditions of knowledge production; that is, she, like language, does not emerge from an Archimedean point or place external to time, geographic space, or other forms of context. The kinds of questions deemed worthy of analysis, the types of sources available for consultation, the concepts that structure ontological and epistemological inquiry, all emanate from particular historical "conditions of possibility." This raises a particular problem for the interpretation of texts or "text-analogues" (evidence of textual OR non-textual kinds), which is how do we use and understand the meaning of the evidence gathered in our research, and how do we understand ourselves in the process?

Philosophers working on this problem from early modernity to the present have developed insights regarding the contextual nature of how we think and understand texts (Benedict de Spinoza in the seventeenth century and Giambatista Vico in the eighteenth), how understanding comes from navigating between the "parts" and "whole" of text or text-analogues (the idea that we cannot understand a given text without situating it in a larger con-text, and that we cannot understand the larger con-text without reference to its parts), how *Erlebnis* (lived tradition) mediates *Verstehen* (understanding) in the work of Wilhelm Dilthey in the nineteenth century, and finally how the researcher's positionality vis-à-vis the text is of central importance for interpretation (Hans-Georg Gadamer in the twentieth century). The researcher, according to Gadamer's development of the hermeneutic circle concept, brings prior experience and knowledge to her reading of the text, which itself is a repository of interpretations over time. The researcher and the text enter into a dialogical relationship that cannot be value-free, because it is conditioned by the respective layers of tradition embodied in each party. Productive interpretation can nevertheless obtain, resulting in a "fusion of horizons" that enables a richer and more textured self-understanding than was previously possible (Ramberg and Gjesdal 2009; Schwartz-Shea and Yanow 2012: 30–31).

Because the researcher is included in the hermeneutic circle, many scholars in IR address the issues it raises for their own participation by insisting on *reflexivity*. This concept concerns the continual analysis of the meaning of the researcher's assumptions, role, and actions in the research process, and incorporates at least part of this reflection into research findings and writings. Much interpretivist ethnographic work, for example, begins with a description of the positionality of the researcher. Feminist work in IR has gone further, acknowledging that both the researcher and research subject's identities, epistemologies (conceptualizations of how knowledge is gained and processed), and worldviews can change during the research process. In some cases, as Maria Stern's work (2006) demonstrates, the researcher's realization of the depth, danger, or precariousness of the research subject's prior, current, or future conditions and of the researcher's own participation in those conditions requires ongoing and ever-deepening reflection about the implications and meaning of the research process itself. As a result, Ackerly and True (2010: 28–30) call for continual attention to the relationships forged and the boundaries that may need to be protected during the research process. For example, reflexivity "may involve interrogating forms of inclusion and exclusion and breaking down boundaries. Likewise it may involve listening for silences and sometimes responsibly sustaining those silences, depending on the context" (Ackerly and True 2010: 29). They, along with Stern, strongly emphasize the necessity of reflexivity, explicating the concept and elevating it to an essential component of "feminist research methodology" (Ackerly, Stern and True 2006).

Power, Ethics, Subjectivity, and Interpretation in the Sub-fields of International Relations

For the field of IR, underdetermination, the symbiotic nature of value and things, the social mediation of reality, the intersubjective nature of institutional practice, and our positionality in the hermeneutic circle all return us to the question of power. Reality is not mediated in most (if any) instances by equality among discursive partners—although international conventions begin from an assumption of formal equality—and mediation does not begin from an Archimedean or external point outside of past and current practices and meanings.[5] Dominant narratives "fill the gaps" between existing forms of evidence and the conclusions drawn from them. As a result, contestations over discursive forms of power and struggles to delegitimize some meanings and create new ones matter.

Interpretation in IR, then, requires a focus on power relationships, including gendered power relationships, which brings with it a sometimes too-implicit focus on ethics. As Cynthia Enloe puts it, understanding the social and gendered nature of power is key: "All of us, as a result, are likely to become much smarter, more realistic about what kinds of power have constructed the international political system as we know it" (Enloe 2000: xviii).

In other words, the corollaries of "knowledge for whom" and "for what purpose" are critical to clarify meanings (Schwartz-Shea and Yanow 2012: 47), because it makes little sense to analyze power relationships without attention to how they came to be, who they benefit, and who they leave out. Interpretivist IR scholars as a result frequently highlight the symbiotic relations between centers of power and theoretical developments in the field (Kurowska and Tallis 2013). IR is a field in which many scholars have close relationships with government and intergovernmental officials, and sometimes become them. From Niccolò Machiavelli to E.H. Carr and Henry Kissinger, theorists have moved in and out of the corridors of governmental power. Others who have not become public officials themselves frequently serve as consultants; still others work to demonstrate the "policy import" of their research, required to do so by foundations and government funders. These relationships between scholarly and "official" forms of power continue to mark all of international relations scholarship in one way or another. They are increasingly complemented and extended by new cohorts of

IR researchers whose relationships with barely "unofficial" channels of power—especially nongovernmental organizations (NGOs)—are equally tight. Scholars of IR, government officials, and NGO representatives together create and replicate terminology and practices that become normative assumptions, guiding both scholarship and policy. The use of terminology such as "democratic peace," "best practices," "sustainable development," and the "responsibility to protect," among others, gives rise to the assumption that particular ideational innovations result in better techniques that, when implemented, can achieve particular policy goals. Interpretivists in IR have consistently argued that the assumptions underlying such terminology and related practices, as well as their construction and implementation by academic and non-academic actors alike, shape and gender world order in particular ways. It is critical to study these relationships, then, to understand how and why some issues and solutions are seen as possible and others as illusory in both academia and government. Disciplinary orthodoxies, in other words, require constant interrogation.

As Stefano Guzzini argues (using "constructivist conceptual analysis" as his starting point), interpretivists are concerned with both what power *means* and what power *does*. Examining and understanding the impact of these "analytical" and "performative" aspects of power, taken together, always show "that a neutral or descriptive meaning of power cannot be found, since the meaning of power is always embedded in a theoretical context; hence conceptual and theoretical analysis interact with each other" (Guzzini 2005: 495 and *passim*). This is why interpretivists very often rely on the work of Michel Foucault in uncovering *discourses* of power; and use a genealogical method to provide a "conceptual history" to show how power has come "to mean . . . and do what it does" (Guzzini 2005: 495). Foucauldian understandings of discourse, as Rabinow emphasizes, encompass both linguistic and "material" artifacts of power, in order to uncover the linkages between terminology, space, architecture, and meaning that allow some forms of knowledge (and hence, power) to dominate during particular periods of time (Rabinow 1984). For example, the move from a discourse of punishment in the medieval era to one of discipline in the modern era entailed changes in forms of bodily and psychological harm, spatial conditions, and moral understandings performed on and attributed to those accused (from public torture to enclosed surveillance) that demonstrates shifts in the techniques, mechanisms, and conceptual understandings of power and order in these periods. The study of the resulting forms of "discursive power" has become critically important for much interpretive research.

Goals and Processes of Interpretive Research in International Relations

These concepts from philosophy of science literatures help us understand the epistemological bases of interpretive research. They do not, in and of themselves, however, tell us what the goals of interpretivist scholars are or how they work to achieve them. Interpretivists in IR aim to accomplish one or more of several types of goals in their research, centering on the Aristotelian notion of *phronesis,* or practical wisdom, rather than tools borrowed from the mathematical sciences. Beyond *phronesis,* interpretivist goals range from *Verstehen* to critique to deconstruction to emancipation.

Social theorists and IR scholars argue about whether the ultimate goal of research is understanding of self, others, or both; or critique, deconstruction, emancipation; or creating some other type of knowledge. Max Weber's concept of *Verstehen* is based on the idea of understanding (rather than, for example, explanation), but takes it further to emphasize the situated and contextualized nature of knowledge construction. *Verstehen,* however, does not necessarily foreground power relations, including the knowledge–power nexus, as a central feature of analysis. Critique, deconstruction, and emancipation, however, each denaturalize and therefore challenge conventional explanations, metanarratives, categorizations, and constructions of power. Critique and emancipation denote a research process that not only seeks to make sense of events, but also more specifically to uncover and expose the workings of dominant forms of power in specific contexts. Deconstruction is generally identified with Jacques Derrida's project of overturning linguistically constructed binary oppositions that enable even everyday violence and exploitation to occur because they emphasize difference and relations of superiority/inferiority (Derrida 1976/97).[6] Michel Foucault's genealogical method, which seeks to analyze and hence expose the techniques and mechanisms of dominant forms of power, can also be seen as a form of deconstruction. Scholars who engage in critique might do so for its own sake or for purposes of deconstruction (in the sense of taking apart the components and binary constructions that form power relations in order to denaturalize them) or they might do so in an attempt to further the emancipation of those who are in some way marginalized, oppressed, or lacking in power. Many scholars who engage in deconstruction, however, are wary of any "reconstructed" power/knowledge nexus, while those, like Gramsci and many feminists, who strive for emancipation seek to expose dominant power relations to open the way to alternatives that are put forth as more equitable or just. Each of these processes emphasizes the importance of the hermeneutic circle, but critique places greater stress on the researcher's responsibility to examine critically the workings of dominant forms of power, deconstruction on the responsibility of the reader of texts or text-analogues to expose the instability of meanings, and emancipation on the responsibility of the scholar/activist to articulate alternatives to inequality and oppression.

Interpretive analysis can also be related to "abduction" and processes of "explication." Both concern the question of how to clarify meaning. Interpretivists use the term abduction, however, to articulate a *form of inference* that is employed when an outcome cannot be explained by available evidence, so the observer must make a lateral move, applying concepts from other, existing fields of knowledge (see Onuf 1989; Friedrichs and Kratochwil 2009; Douven 2011).[7] In this way abduction differs from both deduction and induction. In contrast to induction, which attempts to build knowledge "from the bottom up," those who employ abduction argue that research cannot build in a linear fashion to infer a finding from accumulated evidence, because sometimes an observed result does not logically follow. Induction, moreover, too often relies on the assumptions of the correspondence theory of truth. Interpretivists also argue that deduction, which begins with a general hypothesis about a phenomenon that is difficult to gather information about inductively (for example, a posited but unobservable phenomenon in mathematics or astronomy) and requires the researcher to design empirical "tests" to confirm or disconfirm it, does not allow for the impact of bias in the form of prior knowledge, nor does it take into consideration the implications of historical and spatial contexts. Deduction, in other words, does not recognize the existence or implications of the hermeneutic circle. Both induction and deduction tend to privilege findings of monocausality as the expected outcome of research, while abduction makes no such claims. In working "at an intermediate level" (Friedrichs and Kratochwil 2009: 709), abduction allows for multiple forms of evidence, pathways to scientific discovery, and forms of causality. Abduction, finally, is "concept-driven rather than theory-driven." Thus it is concerned with the constitutive nature of "core concepts," their domains or fields of meaning, and the distinctions among them (Friedrichs and Kratochwil 2009: 716–717).

For interpretivists, then, given that evidence cannot infallibly support unique causes of social phenomena, abductive forms of inference are necessary. Explication, however, connects forms of inference to processes of research and the researcher's intended goals. We might say that abduction as a form of inference relies on the process of explication to demonstrate its logic and hence its reliability. Explication, unlike explanation, seeks to assess the meaning and significance of phenomena or processes, and gain knowledge about their stakes or implications, rather than ascribe causal status to specific variables.[8] According to Rorty, explication moves back and forth between evidence and outcome, working with material (texts and text-analogues) to make sense of it, in specific contexts, in order to respond to the questions animating the research.[9] Explication, then, is an "interpretive process" (Rorty 2004) whose goal is to clarify "the meaning of things" (that which so vexed Michael Palin in the Monty Python sketch).[10] Explication, therefore, works to make "the implicit explicit," with the recognition that implicit knowledge is also "contingent knowledge" (Franklin 2006/2012). As a result, as Schwartz-Shea and Yanow (2012) also assert, the findings, or new knowledge that becomes clearer (through the process of explication) is also subject to further clarification, discussion, and debate. Future research and debates can lead to new interpretations and meanings, because new situations can bring forth different factors to examine or new understandings of events to assess (Franklin 2006/2012).

Finally, "intertextuality" is an important concept in the research process for many interpretivists in IR (Der Derian and Shapiro 1989; Hansen 2006), especially critical theorists and deconstructionists. Intertextuality takes sources, both "high" and "low" (Weldes 2013); both conventional "texts" and "text-analogues" (Taylor 1971/77), and "reads across" them to uncover new meanings, exposing the "'space-between' . . . knowledge and power in international relations" (Yanow 2006: 80; Der Derian and Shapiro 1989). Conventional IR for many decades emphasized the need to gather and evaluate "high data"—documents and interviews from political, military, and economic elites, defense "White Papers," reports and statistics from national and international financial institutions, and treaties and legal accords. All of these remain important for interpretivist IR researchers. However, numerous additional sources of data have become critical for both interpretive and non-interpretive analyses of various kinds. These include websites, reports, and interviews of "non-state" actors, including nongovernmental organizations (NGOs), and interviews, participant-observation, and ethnographies of specific groups of people in particular places (e.g. women in post-conflict situations in Bosnia or El Salvador). Many interpretivists, moreover, increasingly employ "low data" (Weldes 2013), which comprises types of evidence that reflect everyday or elite forms of cultural power, such as film, comics, novels, art, graffiti, or social media including text messages, blogs, and Twitter. How to select among this huge variety of sources (e.g. the "Wayback Machine," a web crawler that archives webpages, includes 150 billion sites!)[11] is beyond the scope of this chapter. However, the necessity of "reading across" even a small selection of this wide variety of sources in order to clarify and uncover meaning makes intertextuality an important interpretive enterprise, especially in genealogies which detail and expose the techniques and mechanisms of power in particular contexts.

Interpretivism in IR, therefore, is characterized by the following features:

- an awareness of the indeterminacy of meaning and an emphasis on contextualization, both of which result in expanded notions of causality (beyond monocausality and ahistorical covering law explanations) to include multicausality, mutual constitution, and contingency;
- a constitutive understanding of fact and value as symbiotically related, resulting in the insight that "truths" are multiple and a single articulation of truth cannot correspond to the totality of "reality";
- an acknowledgement of the importance of the linguistic turn in demonstrating that language conveys meaning instead of providing an exact and objective replica of reality;
- an acknowledgement of the conditioning and positionality of the researcher in articulating some types of questions and not others, and employing some types of assumptions and methodologies and not others, in designing ways to seek knowledge about political and social phenomena;
- an understanding of the existence of the hermeneutic circle, resulting in the need for reflexivity on the part of the researcher regarding his assumptions going into research and his positionality during the research process;
- an awareness and investigation of power in all of the above.

Interpretivist *goals* may represent one or more of the following: *Verstehen*, deconstruction, critique, or the construction of alternatives to the meanings and power relations uncovered and assessed by interpretive research. Researchers accomplish these goals by using abduction as the primary form of inference, explication to clarify and uncover meaning, and intertextuality as a method of reading across texts of "high" and "low" data to expose the connections between power and knowledge, politics and culture.

Each of these aspects of the interpretive enterprise represents an ongoing and evolving practice among interpretive researchers. For example, early interpretive work in IR emphasized the importance of contextuality in shaping interests, identities, and ethics, while more recent research increasingly insists on reflexivity, although just what this requires is still being worked through. In other words, different researchers and types of research in IR lean more heavily on some of these features than others, and interpretivists continue to debate and discuss issues that arise from all of them in the course of their research.

Interpretivism vis-à-vis Positivism and Critical Rationalism

Each of these features also makes interpretive work different from either *positivist* or *critical rationalist* (drawing from Karl Popper's critique of positivism) modes of seeking knowledge (see Hawkesworth 2013 for an excellent analysis). I separate these epistemological stances (rather than, for example, subsuming both under the positivist appellation) for two reasons: 1) following Popperian insights, there are many who assert positivism's demise, and 2) deductive forms of reasoning gained a great deal of disciplinary power in IR, particularly in the subfield of international security, where Kenneth Waltz drew on Karl Popper to assert the necessity of deducing state behavior from properties ascribed to the international system (Waltz 1979). Positivist and critical rationalist epistemologies, which can be quantitative or qualitative in nature, assume that the point of analysis is to specify the relationship between already-constituted variables. Interpretivism calls into question the construction of the variables themselves, and sees their relationship to other factors as fluid rather than having discrete boundaries. For example, rather than looking at the relationship between pre-constituted notions of democracy and peace, a researcher working from interpretive presuppositions could ask how and why democracy is constituted in one way and not another in the late twentieth or early twenty-first century, or how a particular definition of peace as the absence of some forms of conflict and not others was constructed. An exercise that I conduct with students is to ask them to write down the central questions in their research project in two ways, one in the form of hypotheses, the other in the form of a research question focused on meaning. When I ask my students to do this, some have great difficulty doing one or the other, depending on their previous academic experiences and epistemological orientations. We discuss the pros and cons of each; many students remark that hypothesis testing forces them to be specific, but also narrows their question and the means they might use to answer it, as well as predefining factors that they still need to investigate. For interpretive work, we discuss the task of articulating questions that are specific enough to move forward in research and grant-writing, while also allowing flexibility in defining categories of analysis, evaluating a wide range of types of evidence that might be gathered to meet the interpretive requirement of understanding context, and incorporating reflexivity into various stages of the research process. We also, of course, discuss how the character of the research question itself can change according to the epistemological and methodological orientation taken.

This exercise reveals students' socialization experiences into positivist vs. interpretivist assumptions. Positivism prizes parsimony in the expectation that findings can be generalized; interpretivism prizes grappling with complexity and nuance in the expectation that useful insights can be gained and/or "lessons learned" for one or a series of "cases" or historical periods. Positivism and critical rationalism seek law-like formulae or generalizations for relationships between variables;[12] interpretivism emphasizes the idea that the contingent nature of social and political phenomena makes such laws difficult if not impossible. Positivism and critical rationalism assume that researchers can take objective positions outside of the research process; interpretivists assert that the existence of the hermeneutic circle precludes complete objectivity.

Positivist work begins from assumptions of empiricism—the idea that we gain knowledge through progressively (and inductively) gathering and assessing empirical evidence about a phenomenon—while critical rationalism stems from Karl Popper's critique of positivism and relies on deductive forms of inference to formulate testable hypotheses. Interpretive work begins from the assumptions regarding context, indeterminacy, language, and positionality discussed above, and relies more on abductive forms of inference.

Discussing students' socialization experiences also reveals the persistence of a major misconception about interpretive work: that the rejection of the fact/value distinction and the correspondence theory of truth results in anything-goes research with no standards for judging good from poor quality. This misconception should be laid to rest once and for all. Interpretive research, like its positivist and critical rationalist counterparts, can be good or bad. Poor work of any kind makes claims that it cannot sustain according to its own assumptions and methodologies, or that are sloppily supported, or that are either obvious and unoriginal or too easily shot down by alternative explications. Good work is clear about how it addresses its epistemological precepts, thorough in uncovering all available source material (conceptual and/or empirical, depending on the research project), logical and thoughtful in its process of explication, and fair in dealing with alternative understandings and explanations of phenomena and processes. These features of good work make conclusions persuasive, even if they can be further debated.

Many of these features are shared by interpretive, positivist, and critical rationalist work: in other words, these characteristics of good work are agnostic in their ontological and epistemological presuppositions. Where interpretive standards differ is in the requirements placed on the researcher by interpretive epistemological precepts, especially the recognition of the hermeneutic circle and the positionality of the researcher, the acknowledgement of the provisional nature of research findings, the emphasis on the connection between knowledge and power, and the necessity of reflexivity. Interpretivist precepts also mean that the actual research process tends to differ, perhaps more in its conceptualization than in actual fact. The interpretivist insight regarding the implications of the hermeneutic circle, for example, suggests a very different way of approaching research than that of either positivists or critical rationalists. Therefore the research process is not expected to be linear but rather requires explicit and constant tacking back and forth, not only among sources but also regarding the researcher's reflexivity about her initial assumptions vis-à-vis her evidence and findings. While the research process is rarely straightforward in any case, the interpretivist expects and tries to build reflexivity into her research design. Ackerly and True, for example, call for building space for practicing reflexivity into research designs by intentionally engaging in "deliberative moments" at every step of the research process (Ackerly and True 2010).

In conclusion, the philosophy of science that supports interpretive presuppositions, as well as the methodological interventions proposed by interpretivist scholars in IR, is robust and well integrated into canons of logical inquiry and scientific legitimacy. The forms of inference and processes of analysis that guide the methodological interventions proposed by interpretivist scholars in IR build on philosophy of science insights to guide scholars through a variety of research strategies. As a result, interpretive researchers can rely on both precepts and guidelines, as well as already-published research, to articulate and justify the bases of their work. The following chapters demonstrate that such justifications obtain across the subfields of IR, as well as in newly emerging and cross-cutting areas of inquiry.

Notes

1   I use the term nomothetic theorizing to refer to the commitment to finding objective, law-like explanations for phenomena that can be generalized to an entire class of agents.

2   Positivists, moreover, tend to disagree with the assertion that ethics and power are mutually constitutive.

3   This lineage also demonstrates the continued Western biases of IR, including in interpretivist scholarship. Newer work in IR (see Chapter 5) indicates a greater appreciation for the philosophical contributions of Asian and African thought as well.

4   I am indebted to Xymena Kurowska for pointing out the Latin etymology of the word "fact," which is from the verb *facere*, "to do," which connotes action or construction rather than unchanging truth.

5   This is why so much interpretive IR theory is critical of the work of Jürgen Habermas, who articulates a means of "communicative rationality" that begins from a position of equality among interlocutors.

6   Critique and deconstruction can each be considered methods, or groups of methods, but I emphasize here the research goals that are also associated with them.

7   Not all interpretivists in IR conceptualize abduction as a form of inference: I rely on the *Stanford Encyclopedia of Philosophy* to make this case.

8   I do not include emancipation in this part of the discussion because it is more clearly a goal of research rather than a goal and process.

9   In literary criticism, this sense-making concerns the attempt to "explicate" the author's intentions through textual clues and biographical information, among other sources. I am indebted to Nick Onuf for this point. The emphasis here is on the "intentionality" of the "authors" of political processes: state decision-makers, social movements, etc.

10   Explication as a process/goal of research also bridges the alleged gap between "explanation" and "understanding" (Hollis and Smith 1990; Klotz and Lynch 2007). Explanation tends to be the term preferred by positivist analysts, while interpretivists generally seek to understand processes rather than explain the causal relationship between variables.

11   I am enormously indebted to Carrie Reiling and my graduate students for opening this virtual world to me.

12   These are termed "covering laws" and, for positivists, can be falsified through empirical tests.

2

INTERPRETING INTERNATIONAL SECURITY

What is the meaning of security for interpretivists?
How do people and things become secure or insecure?
Who does security benefit and who does it leave out?

Security is a problematic concept for interpretivists in IR. It has long been the primary concern of the IR field, yet its assumptions and ethical implications have been taken for granted in conventional IR rather than problematized and challenged. This chapter explores the longstanding contributions of interpretive scholars in deconstructing, challenging, and reinterpreting what security means and what its ethical and material implications are, for both scholarship and governmental decision-making.

The chapter begins with the "classical realists" in the 1930s, 1940s, and 1950s, who focused on the concerns of traditional diplomacy, including the interplay between morality and power, a problem that is central to this chapter. As IR scholars are by now aware, the "realist" in this appellation refers not to a phenomenological or empiricist concept of reality, but rather to a label taken on by scholars themselves to oppose the "idealism" or "utopianism" that they believed was rampant in attempts to change the world on the part of peace activists and international law experts. These scholars, including E.H. Carr, Reinhold Niebuhr, Hans Morgenthau, Herbert Butterfield, and Martin Wight, among others, believed that academics had to work from a reality defined by the complex of relationships that confronted them rather than what they wanted to engineer for the common good. Classical realists, in other words, brought the thing called "security" to the forefront of international relations scholarship, even as they struggled with its meaning and implications. The complex of relationships that needed to be addressed, in their view, was constituted by moral as well as material meaning and power. As a result, it had to be assessed and acted upon by scholarship and statesmanship informed by virtues of wisdom and prudence.

Classical realists formed the core of "traditional" security studies prior to the positivist behavioral interventions that influenced 1960s peace studies, and the neorealist interventions that formalized the concept of the balance of power into allegedly deductive systems theory. Classical realist precepts then became appropriated by neorealist theory—only to be reappropriated more recently by critical security studies and the "English School" (an approach to IR defined by Dunne 1998, which emphasizes the existence of an "international society" that reflects global norms despite the background condition of anarchy). In tracing aspects of this genealogy, the chapter also engages the seminal work of Arnold Wolfers, one of the early post-World War II "realists" in IR, on the problem of defining the "national interest."

Equally important to interpretive security studies, however, are the contributions of feminist theory to understanding the assumptions underlying the concepts of balance of power and national interest, including their choices, silences, and implications for legitimizing different forms of violence. Critical and postmodern security studies also address these issues, and along with feminism, push forward intertextual investigations of security's meaning, especially reading across gendered experiences and "high" and "low" data (Weldes 2013). The chapter thus examines classical realism, feminist, critical and post-structural work on international security, the "Copenhagen School" of securitization theory, and several new directions in interpretivist security studies in IR.

As discussed in the Introduction, the field of international relations began in earnest in the early twentieth century as part of the Anglo-American Progressive Era's push to professionalize knowledge disciplines in the academy. As we shall see in the forthcoming chapter on international law and organization, international security did not hold the pre-eminent place in the discipline then that it has held more recently, since the beginning of the Cold War. Instead, how to tame war and improve international order through advancing the rule of law motivated much of the creation of the discipline. Nevertheless, questions about the relationship of power to moral order, including military power, were a necessary part of the equation. As the interwar period progressed and the League of Nations became increasingly ineffective, these questions surfaced with greater vigor.

Thinkers and scholars who promoted order through law will be noted in Chapter 4. Those who pushed to the forefront of international relations the issue of whether and when to use military power were the classical realists, as discussed above, and they came largely from the United States and Great Britain. Challenging the primacy of international legal studies after the First World War, they saw the rise of fascism and the outbreak of the Second World War as confirming their arguments about the centrality and endurance of war and conflict in IR.

What were the specific problems, orientations, and methods that allow us to consider them interpretivist? The classical realists understood that different interpretations of foreign policy existed, and insisted on the importance of historical and contextual knowledge for formulating prudential diplomatic and policy positions. There was no agreed-upon scientific toolkit that could generate knowledge in an ahistorical manner; "facts" could not be separated from "values" assigned to foreign policy goals, nor could they trump the orientation, character, and wisdom of policymakers (Alker 1996). Morality and power were fused, and classical realists at least partially explored the interpretive question of *whose* and *what kind* of morality was at stake in specific policy orientations.[1]

The classical realists were concerned with the meaning and importance of what we might call "traditional" diplomacy, including how its forms changed or evolved along with international events. They were also interested in the relationship between values of wisdom and prudence and the exercise of leadership in foreign policy. To what extent could decision-makers maintain control over events, and towards what ends should they do so? Traditional diplomatic history promoted prudence as a primary virtue in the conduct of foreign policy. To be prudent was to marry wisdom to knowledge of the world gained by both historical study and experience. Prudence in diplomacy (Loriaux 1992; Lebow 2007) usually favored accruing military might, but it did not necessarily entail using it by going to war. Nor could prudence ensure sufficient control over adversaries' ideational or material capacities to cause events to turn out in one's favor. The classical realists, therefore, did not conceptualize causality rigidly. More importantly, they privileged the possession of wisdom by diplomats and leaders, in addition to broad-based historical knowledge, so that they would be able to respond to unforeseen contingencies. If combined with an astute understanding of the workings of the balance of power, prudential decision-making would result in the protection of national interests.

The terms balance of power and national interests, of course, beg further questions for contemporary interpretivists, as they did for classical realists and scholars of international law and organization. Several well-known books and articles examined the variety of definitions and meanings of the term "balance of power," for example, noting that it could refer either to the description of actual power relationships at any given time, or a prescription for a particular type of balance that would privilege some interests over others, and that these definitions suggested different strategies for knowledge construction and policy (Claude 1962; 1989). While later theorists employed the term to denote a constant state of affairs or the structural distribution of military power in particular systemic eras in international politics, diplomatic studies that related description to prescription underpinned the concerns of classical realists. The concern of the classical realists, in other words, was to understand the nature of shifting balances historically—what made them shift? how was power used or misused? what moves proved prudent or imprudent?—as a means of evaluating their contemporary situation, and through this knowledge act in prudential fashion to increase national power and influence where possible. Usually, acting prudently required maintaining a balance, but if contextual factors changed, it could instead mandate the attempt to undermine or change a situation of perceived "imbalance" to one more in a particular state's favor.

Balances should be either maintained or changed, according to diplomatic historians, to shore up or protect the national interest. What that interest entailed, however, aside from protecting the existence and boundaries of the nation–state, was debatable. To what degree moral vision should be considered an integral component of the national interest along with maintaining or increasing military and economic capabilities, for example, was a major component of classical realist security debates.

E.H. Carr (1939/46) maintained that power and moral purpose were both necessary components of both the national interest and global order, although for many commentators he emphasized the former over the latter (Bull 1969; Smith 1987; Lynch 1999, 2000). For Carr, Wight, Butterfield, Morgenthau, and Niebuhr, the power of right moral purpose was incalculable. The lesson they drew from diplomatic history was that the blatant use of power for immoral reasons resulted in at best pyrrhic victories. More frequently, such immoral use robbed a state of the legitimacy and authority needed to promote its interests in the world.

Some classical realists, especially Hans Morgenthau, addressed reason, rationality, and science in ways that would eventually be claimed by positivist as well as interpretive scholars. J. Ann Tickner, for example, points out that Hans Morgenthau wanted to advance "science" over "ideology" because of how he interpreted his own historical positionality as a scholar who experienced the rise of fascism: "Flagrant violations of international law and abuses of human rights in the name of German nationalism motivated Morgenthau, and other early realists, to dissociate the realm of morality and values from the realpolitik of international politics." Such experiences made ideologically determined perspectives of the world dangerous; Morgenthau's resort to "science" was at least in part an attempt to find other, more rational grounds for analyzing the causes of war and decreasing its likelihood (Tickner 1997: 618; see also Williams 2004 and Lebow 2003). Morgenthau, however, struggled with the meaning and importance of science for analyzing security, demonstrated by his critique, detailed in *Scientific Man vs. Power Politics,* of the liberal rationalist's application of the methodologies of the physical sciences to analyze and explain social phenomena (Morgenthau 1946; see also Turner and Oren 2009 on the Weberian methodological foundations of Morgenthau's thought). This critique paralleled that of E.H. Carr, who rejected liberals' attempts to create a peaceful world order through processes of social engineering, such as promoting world peace through international law and global international organization.

The primary solution to the dangers of fanaticisms of all kinds was the use of reason and the rational assessment of political contexts. Prudence could not obtain without reason and rationality, which could channel if not tame the will to power that was an essential characteristic of human nature. Reason and rationality, however, despite their position at the pinnacle of virtues that leaders should possess, could not be decoupled from historical context. As a result, after the Second World War, Morgenthau's work (exemplified in the classic *Politics Among Nations*) represented "'a frontal attack'" on "the liberal view that power politics is something that can eventually be suppressed" (Morgenthau 1978: xiii; Cozette 2008: 670). Later, however, his emphasis on assessing the national interest in terms of power evolved, and he began to insist more strongly on morality and legitimacy as essential components of power. During the Vietnam War, for example, he warned that the United States had suffered a severe loss in prestige that negated its "'transcendent purpose,'" which was to achieve "'equality in freedom'" (Morgenthau 1960: 8, quoted in Cozette 2008: 670). Politics, then, was not merely a struggle for power after all, and the "national interest" required attention to moral values and transcendent purpose as well as conventional understandings of power politics (Lang 2004: 111; cited in Cozette 2008: 670–671; see also Williams 2005).[2]

Classical realists, then, exhibited faith in prudence, reason, and rationality to promote wise foreign policy leadership, even if they did not believe that either anarchy or the will to power in international politics could be overcome. They also understood decision-making as conditioned by historical, geographic, and moral factors. Taken together, these two commitments resulted in thoughtful commentary on the content of the national interest. While Hans Morgenthau could go so far as to define interest in terms of power (Morgenthau 1978: 4–15), E.H. Carr continually pointed out that both interest and power were conditioned by ideology and historical context. Reinhold Niebuhr went farther in his moral critique to deplore many of the policies presumably resulting from interest, individual or national, which he articulated in terms of "selfishness" (Niebuhr 1932/2002).

Arnold Wolfers, however, wrote one of the best interpretive exposés on the national interest concept. Published in 1952 in the journal *Political Science Quarterly,* Wolfers' treatment of the ambiguity of the national interest became a classic. Wolfers evaluates the substantive and moral claims of the "national interest" and extends it to the concept of "national security." He finds both problematic to pin down: "They may not mean the same thing to different people. They may not have any precise meaning at all. Thus, while appearing to offer guidance and a basis for broad consensus they may be permitting everyone to label whatever policy he favors with an attractive and possibly deceptive name" (Wolfers 1952: 481). Wolfers acknowledges that the national interest does connote the good of the *nation,* rather than that of other forms of collective political organization, and asserts that, at his time of writing, interest tended to be tied to conceptions of national security as freedom from external military threat rather than the accumulation or fairer distribution of wealth. But, in the classical tradition of evaluating morality along with threat, and recognizing the existence of competing values, he also argues that any definition of national security requires an estimation of what sacrifices are moral and bearable versus what types of military preparedness might actually provoke threatening responses, including arms races. While written in the early days after the Second World War, Wolfers' ability to contextualize conceptions of national interest and security for his own era as well as compare them to those of other eras is a model of good interpretivist scholarship in the classical realist tradition.

Classical realists, then, put interpretive issues of contextual meaning, the symbiosis of fact and value, and the importance of language and perception at the core of their work. Yet they tended to agree that some types of power—especially military—were more critical than others for states who wanted to act persuasively in international relations. They also agreed that what used to be called the "high politics" of state security (Weldes 2013) should supersede other foreign as well as domestic policy considerations. Even Reinhold Niebuhr, who deplored many aspects of great power machinations and considered the use of force to be an "evil" (although at times the better of two evils), concurred with these conclusions, and provided moral cover for them under the guise of distinguishing between the appropriate moral constraints on the individual versus the group (Niebuhr 1932/2002). Classical realists continued to inform scholarship on security into the 1960s and 1970s, when Morgenthau and Niebuhr opposed the Vietnam War. Non-interpretivist competitors, however, including peace researchers intent on quantifying the relative impact of factors leading to peace or war, levels-of-analysis theorists who wished to specify whether the "necessary and sufficient" causes of war should be conceptualized as individual, state or international systemic factors, and eventually neo-realists such as Kenneth Waltz who were committed to deductive analyses in the tradition of Karl Popper, increasingly took over the "mainstream" of the subfield.

Feminist Security Studies

While (predominantly male) security scholars argued about the causes of war, feminist theorists began to challenge the classical realists' focus on military power and diplomacy as the best methods for ensuring security, the positivist and neorealist definitions of the national interest and the silences of both regarding the forms of violence perpetrated by policies that resulted from such emphases, assumptions, and definitions. At a minimum, such an exclusive focus on the balance of power and the use of force to protect the national interest reinforced masculinist values, taking them for granted and denying the experiences, roles, and perspectives of women. At a maximum, a statist focus ignored how violence connects the family, domestic/state, and international levels of society (Tickner 1992; Peterson and Runyan 1999: 116). Many feminists also challenged the primacy of the state itself. Indeed, state interactions were structured to promote gendered interests, defined as "high politics," with the resort to force normalizing militarism while ignoring its effects on women's lives. The next chapter addresses feminists' concerns about domestic as well as global relations of production and their effects on gender; for now what is important is that feminists have consistently insisted on analyzing the gendered economic, social, and cultural implications of militarism.

As Chapter 1 indicates, writers who lived contemporaneously with the classical realists, including Virginia Woolf and Jane Addams, among others, deplored the lack of attention in foreign policy to the conditions of women, families, and "domestic" concerns. Feminist peace theorists such as Elise Boulding took on these among other issues in the 1970s, challenging the classical realist pessimism regarding human nature by observing that many people, including women and people of different cultures, act out of collaborative and nurturing motivations instead of a will to power (Confortini 2012). While most feminists reject the claim that women are inherently more nurturing or less violent than men, and assert instead that both gender and its effects on violence are socially constructed, scholars such as Cynthia Enloe began to bring women directly into the very definition of security by studying the unseen or ignored implications of militarism on their lives. Enloe's pathbreaking and detailed empirical work on the conditions and subjective positions of women that resulted directly from security politics, policies and frameworks highlighted the interpretivist insight that positionality matters for both researchers and research subjects. Enloe was especially careful not to neglect power. Indeed, gendered relations of power formed the foundation of her work. "We are . . . coming to realize that the traditional concepts of masculinity and femininity have been surprisingly hard to perpetuate; it has required the daily exercise of power—domestic power, national power, and . . . international power" (Enloe 1989/2000: 3). As Enloe pointed out, the intersection of these forms of power produced rampant prostitution at military bases (especially in the Third World) and required the constant work of diplomatic wives to keep the machinery of foreign policy humming (also see Enloe 1993 as well as many other subsequent books). The gendered implications of security frameworks and policies also had racial and ethnic analogues, frequently suggested by Enloe and other feminists but explored more fully in later work. Enloe's research, nevertheless, along with the second wave of feminist theorizing in the 1990s, served to open the floodgates of feminist work on security, culminating today in a growing body of research on the intersections of race, class, religion, and ethnicity as well as gender (explored in Chapter 5).

J. Ann Tickner and Jean Bethke Elshtain, among others, next began to pose direct challenges to core assumptions of IR theory. Tickner, for example, took on Hans Morgenthau's "principles of political realism" (Tickner 1988) to demonstrate how the very definition of power by realists such as Morgenthau, "the control of man over man," and the separation of the "political" sphere (already focusing on military might) from the economic and the social, embodied "masculine" assumptions. These assumptions, taught as fact, have become naturalized when they should be interrogated (Tickner 1988: 431–434). Incorporating feminist considerations, however, necessitates a reformulation of these taken-for-granted assumptions. Once this is done, the very definition of security changes in fundamental ways: for example, concepts such as the "national interest" must be thought of in cooperative as well as competitive terms. As Tickner and Sjoberg explain, "IR feminist theories focus on social relations, particularly gender relations; rather than anarchy, they see an international system constituted by socially constructed gender hierarchies which contribute to gender subordination" (Tickner and Sjoberg 2007: 187–188). Feminists, then, challenge taken-for-granted security constructs on the basis of lived experience, and trace the mutual impact of local/individual/familial and national/transnational conceptions of security and conflict (see also Wibben 2011).

Elshtain challenged theory from a different perspective, showing how the tropes of men's idealization as the "just warrior" and women's as the "beautiful soul" ("a collective being embodying values and virtues that are at odds with war's destructiveness, representing home and hearth and the humble verities of everyday life": Elshtain 1987/95: xiii) are in effect social, literary, and historical constructions that permeate feminist and anti-feminist rhetoric alike. She details stories that highlight the permutations of these images to demonstrate how they shape and delimit gendered identities. Moreover, she challenges both feminists and their critics to think through the implications of these constructions in order to assess the possibility of moving beyond them.

These and other feminists demonstrate that not only the lives of women, but the multiplicity of feminist theoretical insights needed to be incorporated into security studies. Not only are wars fought partly out of the myth that women and children need protection, but these same populations constitute huge numbers of casualties, especially in contemporary warfare. (This myth of protection extends today to arguments in favor of humanitarian intervention, bolstered by the promotional materials of nongovernmental organizations which portray women and children as passive victims in need of assistance.) Knowledge, however, benefits when a reflexive sensibility is inculcated into thinking through both the presuppositions and imagery encountered in research. When these characteristics become part of the research process on international security issues, the very foundations of what it means to be secure and how men and women think about war and peace change, reflecting the interpretivist insight that the symbiotic nature of fact and value propel knowledge creation and social interaction.

Feminist work, moreover, opened new questions for both IR theory and the subfield of international security, including whose interests were at stake in masculinizing security studies and what specifically could be gained by developing feminist perspectives. Most feminist IR scholars clearly articulated their goal to improve the political and economic conditions of women, a focus that would help transform the concept of "national security" to "human security" and more recently "gender security." Thus their overall goal was emancipatory (one of the goals of interpretive research discussed in Chapter 1). But the weight of the argument that gender had been suppressed in the field of IR incorporated many other interpretive assumptions and concerns. Perspectives and interpretations of what was important in security policies could and did vary according to place, time, and now gender; the national interest was not a given, and experiential (phenomenological) contexts mattered a great deal. IR theory could not be complete without incorporating women's voices, both empirical and theoretical, which had heretofore been absent.

These arguments also begged questions of language and discourse. Carol Cohn's pathbreaking participant-observation in a nuclear weapons thinktank showed how gendered discursive constructions of the most destructive kinds of "technostrategic warfare" worked to denigrate characteristics considered to be feminine, emotional, or ethical, instead promoting masculinist terminology and stereotypes that masqueraded as "rational" and "detached" (Cohn 1987; Confortini 2006). Cohn explored the highly charged sexualization of both nuclear weapons and nuclear strategy, demonstrating how the ensuing social constructions helped (male) nuclear scientists to disengage themselves from the effects of nuclear weapons' use on real men and women and arrive at analyses that precluded the possibility of other ethical constructions of nuclear weapons or strategies. Cohn also pushed forth the self-reflexive stance taken by earlier feminists by exploring her own socialization into sexualized discourse and imagery. In fact, she speaks of the "terror" of recognition when she stopped working at the lab and had time to assess the implications of her participation on her own attitudes and discursive practices (Cohn 1987; see also Klotz and Lynch 2007). The idea of terror in this case is a prime example of reflexively analyzing the research process and one's own positionality in it: Cohn speaks of her terror when, upon achieving some temporal and geographic distance from the nuclear weapons lab, she recognized just how comfortable she had become with assumptions and terminology she had initially found shocking, phallic, and illogical (see also Cohn 2006).

Despite the innovative and compelling nature of feminist arguments regarding the theory and practice of international security, the backlash against them was strong. As Lene Hansen pointed out, many women were still "prevented from being subjects worthy of speaking" (Hansen 2000): or if they spoke, they were often not taken seriously. Charges, mainly by positivists, that gender studies represented personal attacks against men, and/or that feminist ontologies and epistemologies were invalid and did not address "real" security questions and issues, were leveled at feminist security theorists, prompting J. Ann Tickner to draw on a title from a well-known book by Deborah Tannen to publish an article entitled, "You Just Don't Understand" (Tickner 1997). Informed by "fairly widely shared experiences that I and other feminist scholars have had when speaking to IR audiences" (p.612; fn 5), Tickner described a "gendered estrangement" that produced these charges against feminist theorists' research on security (Tickner 1997: 613). The debate between feminist and "mainstream" theorists also demonstrated the personal stakes and investment in scholarly identity that are constitutive of the research process. When reflexivity about these stakes is absent, legitimate concerns and insights of feminist research are dismissed, and ontological and epistemological estrangement, misunderstandings, and even violence (in the sense of silencing critical conceptualizations by feminist theorists as well as empirical findings about

women and men in specific global contexts) can result. Even critical security
theorists have minimized the importance of feminist work, both by perpetuating
gendered assumptions and by committing a sin of omission in talking to each
other while ignoring feminist work and its insights (Hansen 2000; see Sylvester 2007 for a trenchant exposition of disciplinary gendering in critical security
theory).[3] Such omissions continue today, demonstrating the problematic nature of
the correspondence theory of truth as well as the importance of the researcher's
positionality in the hermeneutic circle.

The "second generation" of feminist international security scholars, including Jacqui True (2003), Charlotte Hooper (2001), and many others, has focused
on integrating these theoretical insights into empirical studies of how war and
militarism affect gender relations in many parts of the world (see also Stern 2006
and D'Costa 2006), and for particular forms of weapons and militarism (Kinsella
2011). This work, especially the experiences of interviewing women who had
lived through the violence of war and rape, prompted many new questions regarding the meaning and practice of reflexivity (on reflexivity in feminist work,
see Chapter 1). Brooke Ackerly, Maria Stern, and Jacqui True have since articulated a "feminist methodology" that is largely interpretivist in nature and is designed
to inform not only security but also other subfields in IR. The concept of "im-
manent critique" (Ackerly, Stern and True 2006: 244) denotes a shared field of
inquiry and constant reflexivity on the part of the researcher that incorporates
the research subject. In the field of security studies, scholars using this concept are
particularly attentive to the multiple forms of exclusion and violence experienced
by women. Ongoing debate among feminists regarding how to think about and
conceptualize security itself, including human security, gender security, holistic
security, and feminist security (Shepherd 2010; Wibben 2011), indicates that feminist theorists' methodology of continual interrogation contributes to preventing
international security from becoming reified in interpretive IR.

In many ways, feminist interpretive work on international security today continues to probe the set of questions outlined by Christine Sylvester in 1994:

> 'How can we simultaneously put women at the center and decenter ev-
> erything including women' (K. Ferguson 1993: 3)? How can we bring
> women into view and valorize their experiences while casting a skeptical
> eye on gender identities worn like birthday suits? Can we have meaning-
> ful identities and question them too or must we choose between identity
> and resistance to identity? Can we theorize 'the subject as *produced* through
> signifying practices which precede her' (Ebert 1988: 23), while also granting
> personal and social significance to some of those produced practices?
> *(Sylvester 1994: 12–13)*

Sylvester asserts that "postmodern feminism" (as opposed to feminist postmod-
ernism, whose first commitment is to the second term) can answer some of these

questions productively. This is because, similar to the methodology outlined by Tickner, Ackerly, Stern, and True (and Robinson in Chapter 4), it

> homesteads through a radically empathetic conversational politics that helps us to learn the strengths and limitations of our inherited identity categories and to decide our identities, theories, politics, and daily concerns rather than continue to derive them from, or reject them out of hand because they come from, established authority sources.
>
> *(Sylvester 1994: 14)*

Sylvester calls for "a method of empathetic cooperation to elicit the subjectivities of 'women', . . . of 'really listening to what others say . . . attempting to incorporate those views into [our] own [so that we] become somewhat transformed by that incorporation'" (Hirschmann 1992: 252; in Sylvester 1994: 14).

As the discussion of Spivak indicates in the next chapter, there are significant obstacles in the way of this goal, especially given interpretivist insights about the researcher's positionality and the existence of the hermeneutic circle, but feminist scholars continue to explore ways to achieve greater reflexivity, understanding, and transformation regarding the exclusions that lie at the heart of conventional security concepts. Moreover, it is clear that feminist methodologies, research ethics, and insights regarding reflexivity, along with feminists' insistence on gender as constitutive of international relations and international security, have all been influential in shaping interpretive work regarding the meaning and content of security, as well as the gendered implications of knowledge construction in the subfield.

Critical Security Studies

While feminist perspectives proliferated and provoked strong reactions in the field, a new genre now referred to as "critical security studies" began to take hold. The premises of critical security studies include the idea that what constitutes "security" cannot be taken for granted, nor can any statement regarding whose security is most important be taken at face value. As the editors of the1997 volume that gave the genre its name state, "To be a member of the security studies community has traditionally meant that one already *knows* what is to be studied. Both the object of security (what is to be secured) and the means for studying it are treated as largely given and self-evident" (Krause and Williams 1997). Moreover, any deviation from this norm is not only viewed as unconstructive but also as destabilizing by scholars of conventional security studies. Taking a prototypical example, the editors assert that one well-known security expert "seems to argue that one of the biggest threats to security is the seductive appeal of contrary methods for understanding it" (Williams and Krause 1997: ix). This self-reinforcing tendency to study pre-fixed concepts and relationships that cannot be questioned precludes central interpretivist tenets of positionality and reflexivity, and ignores the insights obtained from critical theory regarding the symbiotic relationship between knowledge and power, as well as those from the linguistic turn regarding the constitutive power of discourse and the absence of any distinction between fact and value. Thus, according to critical security theorists, conventional international relations and the international security subfield are historically too bound up with state leaders and their interests: not only are the topics of analysis already formed and taken-for-granted, but many academics specializing in security studies move in and out of the foreign policy, military, and intelligence communities. While such government service might produce critiques of specific foreign policies, these most often center on tactical issues and rarely challenge the central belief that security requires the ability of the state to make war. At issue, once again, are the social construction of knowledge and the power relationships among scholars and state authorities.

Prior to the coining of the term "critical security studies," scholars such as James Der Derian (1987) and David Campbell (1992) published major works that deconstructed the diplomatic and military underpinnings of assumptions central to IR. Using combinations of Marx on alienation, Nietzsche on genealogy, Foucault on discursive power, and Derrida on difference, they along with others demonstrated the techniques of power, both disciplinary and discursive, that produced conventional understandings of the state, sovereignty, and the strategic balance of power. A central aim of this work was to engage in critique and deconstruction, disrupting the naturalization of neorealist and neoliberal theory by probing the intertext between power and knowledge and exposing its discursive construction, rather than to develop "better" policy in favor of either peace or war (see also Ashley 1988; George 1994; and Dillon 1996).

What eventually developed as critical security studies drew on this work to insist on the necessity and legitimacy of interrogating the meaning of security and destabilizing its rigid adherence to a fixed notion of the state. As a result, the first generation of critical security theorists called into question what appeared to be "natural" state security interests. Some prescient critical security theorists also drew on feminist theory to raise "the difficult question of what is being secured." As Simon Dalby asserted, the "feminist arguments that security (in terms of masculinist modes of domination) secures patriarchal relations of power and renders women insecure precisely because they are women undercuts the state-centric logic of the security discourse" (Dalby 1997: 7).

Ken Booth offers an introspective analysis of the development of critical security perspectives, as one of several former "mainstream" UK security theorists who grew increasingly disillusioned by the contradictions in the theory and practice of security in the nuclear era; this group also included Steve Smith and Michael Dillon. Appealing to the feminist insight that "the personal is political," Booth illustrates the development of critical security insights by relating the story of his own socialization into conventional security studies and his gradual questioning of the illogics involved. While talking to a peace group "about such realist truisms as the 'inescapable' war system, the 'impossibility' of disarmament, the 'rational' relationship between military power and national security, the 'perpetual' nuclear peace, the 'just' nuclear deterrent, and this as 'the best of all possible worlds'," he began to view his own dictums as irrational social constructions. As a result, he redefined security as "cultural" rather than structural (Booth 1997: 99–100).

Extending this type of reflexivity to broader audiences is one of the goals of critical security theory. Weldes, Laffey, Gusterson and Duvall, for example, examine the relationship between "culture" and "security" as a contested concept (1999: 1), arguing that "insecurities, rather than being natural fact, are social and cultural productions" (1999: 10). Arguing that there is nothing given about security, and relating security to culture, also opens the door to denaturalizing accepted definitions of allies and enemies and allowing for the possibility of alternatives. "Security imaginaries," in this view, become identified as rational state interests, a concept which becomes difficult to sustain logically, as Wolfers argued half a century before. Jutta Weldes demonstrates how U.S. elites appealed to four discursively constituted aspects of identity ("as global and hemispheric leader, as the bastion and defender of freedom, as strong and resolute, and as credible") to create a security imaginary that represented Soviet intermediate-range nuclear missiles sent to Cuba as a defining "crisis" and existential threat to U.S. security in October of 1962 (Weldes 1999: 41). Scholars of critical security studies also move beyond Western constructions of threat to ask how other states and regions articulate the relationship among identity, culture, and security. Himadeep Muppidi, for example, asks why India's relationship with the United States during the Cold War was more fraught than its relationship with the former Soviet Union. He argues that conventional security studies miss the meaning of India's postcolonial anxieties vis-à-vis the West and particularly vis-à-vis U.S. hegemony. Muppidi "offers an alternative answer based on an interpretive conceptualization of Indian security policy as shaped around a specific postcolonial security imaginary," and constituted by a "limited set of social practices" that mark its boundaries (Muppidi 1999: 120).

The concept of security imaginaries, then, indicates how particular meanings produce and organize power in specific ways. Security imaginaries promote the articulation of some identities over others, and "hail" or "interpellate" broader segments of the citizenry into these constructions by mobilizing a variety of discursive forms (i.e. evidence), including visual imagery, official statements and public pronouncements, and the manipulation of media sources, among others. Muppidi, Weldes, Duvall, and other "critical constructivist" security theorists describe these processes according to insights from Foucault (on discursive power) and Louis Althusser (on the concept of interpellation).

The studies above beg once again the question of language, including how concepts that evoke emotion (safety, threat, freedom) are deployed to create feelings of trust, fear, or moral superiority. The broader discourses in which such terms are embedded supports and naturalizes the reproduction of dominant techniques of power (the constant production of new generations of weapons, the push for technological innovations in surveillance techniques, etc.) over possible alternatives. Demonstrating how the "material" aspects of these forms of power are constructed and embedded in ongoing discursive practices is a major task of much critical security work.

Some interpretivist security scholars take these insights in a somewhat different direction, by focusing on how ensembles of actors participate in discursive systems of rules. Drawing from the later Wittgenstein's insight that language reflects meaning rather than faithfully representing "reality," Karen Fierke (1998, 2001) demonstrates how actors, or "players," engage in "language games" that shape their actions ("moves") vis-à-vis each other. As Friedrich Kratochwil argues, signaling between adversaries cannot take place without intersubjective understanding and adherence to rules (Kratochwil 1989). The Cuban Missile Crisis of 1962, as well as the Cold War arms race and arms control processes, are examples that demonstrate the complexity of language games, including how signaling, negotiations, threats and retreats were played out by the United States and the former Soviet Union against a normative background and "rules of the game" tacitly agreed to by both parties.

The ultimate focus of this type of analysis differs, as Fierke points out, from the poststructuralist emphasis on denaturalization and deconstruction. "Poststructuralists . . . have argued that *a priori* meanings, rather than *a priori* rationality, provide the backdrop for action" (Fierke 2001: 123). But "the concept of a game provides another way to think about the relationship between [constructions of] rationality and structures of meaning." A game is relational, requiring interaction with others, but unlike the games of rational choice theorists, this type of interpretivist game connotes "a structure of rules within which identities and practices are given meaning" (Fierke 2001: 123). The players—and the analyst—must know the rules of the game to understand the meaning assigned to the discourse and actions of self and others. Moreover, in most cases there is more than one game going on at the same time, but they occur in the same "intersubjective space" and therefore overlap. Rules encode meaning in each of these games, providing the context in which actors' moves appear logical and rational. Thus, for example, if we want to understand the end of the Cold War, we must identify both the rules of the dominant game and the "larger intersubjective context" to see how moves that might shift the game toward alternatives might seem "reasonable and therefore justifiable" (Fierke 2001: 125). Ronald Reagan and most U.S. government actors felt trapped in the logic of the security dilemma, but Mikhail Gorbachev's moves reflected a new, more collaborative game that was being played simultaneously and eventually enabled new rules of the game to gain ascendancy.

In later work on violent acts of self-destruction that are variously described as "suicide bombing" or "martyrdom," Fierke describes two different discursive "games," one based on each term, that have been played in the war on terror. Again, each rests on multiple cultural constructions, but is also constitutive of the other in the broader intersubjective "space" in which debates take place about the legitimate grievances, means and goals of actors (Fierke 2009). The goal of this framework is first to engage in *Verstehen* through processes of explication, but second to create discursive openings that make policy change possible. Denaturalization, here, is an essential prerequisite but not the ultimate objective of research:

> Questioning the assumptions upon which the current logic of violence rests is a first step. . . . A second step is to recognize how the Western response to suicide terrorism has fed the widespread sense of injustice and humiliation, which has in turn fed 'martyrdom' among Arab and Muslim populations. . . . A third step is to refocus the problem and the solution on the humanitarian issues and loss of dignity that underpin the public emotions and the structural logic generated by both sides.
>
> *(Fierke 2009: 180)*

The language games approach, as a result, differs from deconstructionist work as well as some critical security studies in proposing a new type of "game" to replace the ones played previously.

Critical security literature does not, however, focus only on the more apparent trappings of militarism (weapons of mass destruction; modes of engendering terror) apparent in neorealist strategic assumptions. It also works to denaturalize the allegedly more pacific constructs underlying U.S. hegemony in a liberal world order. More specifically, the "democratic peace" literature, which claims that democracies are less likely to fight each other than non-democracies, became a cottage industry during the 1990s and its terminology was taken up and repeatedly touted by elites including former President Bill Clinton. Even though Michael Doyle had warned that democracies are not necessarily peace-loving, carrying out wars of aggression against "illiberal" states (Doyle 1996), the appeal of the democratic peace concept to a global power that prided itself on the moral rightness of its causes and that could not reconcile its moral stance with defeat in Vietnam gave it an enormous discursive boost. Doyle's insights, while still "liberal" in the sense of retaining the hope of progress, became vastly oversimplified (Lynch 1994).

Ido Oren's work on the relationship between the growth of U.S. power and the assumptions guiding the work of political scientists in the post-World War II era—assumptions that culminated in the democratic peace thesis—is instructive for bringing a critical approach to the literature. Oren, among other things, studied the data sets that scholars used to support the democratic peace argument. He found that *a priori* assumptions guided both the categorization and accumulation of data and the resulting conclusions, resulting in the very type of tautological argument that both inductive and deductive theorizing in principle reject as invalid (Oren 2003: 179). More specifically, Oren argues that "democracy" is a linguistic convenience for "America-like."

The definition of democracy (that is, US) manifest in the data sets employed by international relations scholars is the product of a subtle historical process in which . . . those aspects of the concept that made US resemble our enemies have been discarded, while those dimensions that magnified the distance between US and our enemies have become privileged.

(Oren 2003: 179)

What is to be done? Oren calls for a "reflexive approach," but in a sense that differs somewhat from feminist theorists. While the latter address the differential relations of power and experience that occur between the researcher and her subjects of study, Oren calls on the discipline of political science to be self-conscious in addressing the relationship between "its own scholarship" and "historical political processes" (Oren 2003: 178). Democratic peace scholarship, according to this approach, should be viewed

as a part of, rather than apart from, the very historical process of international politics on which it purports to shed light. For example, rather than study 'the fact of democratic peace,' as students of international relations commonly do, this type of reflexivity directs us to inquire into the history of the analytical concepts, including 'democracy,' which the discipline uses to measure, classify, and order its 'facts.'

(Oren 2003: 178)

The mandate to acknowledge one's position in the hermeneutic circle is clear; while there is no Archimedean point from which to begin to analyze "democracy" as a concept, it is possible to examine its conditions of possibility and its implications in different historical contexts. Refusing to accept this mandate, for critical security scholars, once again obscures the many forms of violence that result from conventional security precepts.

Not only is the notion of "democratic culture" problematic, but, as many interpretivist IR scholars agree, so are the concepts of the state and sovereignty. R.B.J. Walker problematized both in his classic book *Inside/Outside* (1993), which challenged the primacy of the state by tracing its conceptualization by political theorists from early modernity to the late twentieth century. Walker demonstrates that the state emerged through this discursive history, rendering other forms of political community unimaginable and reinforcing the meaning of security as concerning almost exclusively the state (see also Walker 1990).

Tarak Barkawi and Mark Laffey take the critique of the state in a different direction in analyzing what they call "embedded statism"—the reification of the state in both conventional IR theory and foreign policy—as problematic historically as well as theoretically. Like Oren, they challenge the findings of liberal peace theory, but they do so by charging that the very definitions of "war" as well as of "democracy" are fluid rather than static. If this is the case, we can see that it does not much matter for peace and war whether "democracies" refrain from targeting each other militarily. This is because during the Cold War (and after), "liberal" or "democratic" states have wielded enormous power in peripheral, "client" states, which "took on central importance as the site of armed conflict" (Barkawi and Laffey 1999: 410). But this is not merely a question of displacing conflict to the periphery: while conventional security experts focus on the "enforced peace" between the major powers during the Cold War, Barkawi and Laffey argue that the use of clients and proxies in peripheral states by major powers (which are also former colonial powers) changed the nature of war itself and the geography of citizen participation. "[T]he forces of only one superpower could become engaged in any particular locality and both sides resorted to various forms of raising troops from foreign, client populations." The superpowers "supplied, trained, advised and often directed" their client forces in battle, even though in the democratic peace data, such client forces are coded as belonging completely to peripheral "states." As a result, both "democracy" and "war" become fluid categories (Barkawi and Laffey 1999: 410).

If one insight from philosophers of science is that social outcomes are underdetermined (see Chapter 1), Barkawi and Laffey, among others, point out that the very character and content of allegedly fixed social phenomena also changes over time. That is to say, not only are cause/effect relationships impossible to determine with finality, but the things that are being related (which causes and which effects) are also fluid, without fixed meanings.

The assumption that fixed and unchanging variables relate to each other in ways that produce law-like outcomes that can be described in ahistorical fashion can also result in problematic policy decisions. David Campbell analyzed how assumptions about fixed and unchanging ethnic identities on the part of Western power brokers led to the Dayton Accords that were supposed to resolve the problem of violence in Bosnia. Campbell argues that identities before the war were fluid, but that Western powers actually fed into the narratives of ethnic separatism pushed by those who engaged in ethnic cleansing (Campbell 1998). The reification of assumptions about ethnic identity led to policies that assumed that Bosnian Muslims, Croats, and Serbs could never get along and must be separated, resulting in an uneasy "peace" that prevented rather than enabled ethnic and religious pluralism and syncretism.

A major implication of each of these studies is that scholarship has consequences because it can produce or reinforce assumptions that push to the forefront some outcomes while delegitimizing others. Those interpretations that "win" cannot be verified as true, and evidence demonstrating that they are constructed from problematic assumptions and variables is often bountiful. Yet because they are continually reinforced discursively and supported by specific military, media, and/ or policy strategies, they become naturalized as "fact," and other policy options appear impossible to imagine, let alone achieve. Understanding and probing this insight is why many interpretivist IR scholars are reluctant to propose alternative policies, instead insisting that critique and deconstruction are the most powerful forms of research. This is also why many critical security scholars focus on the question of *how* particular outcomes are made possible instead of *why* particular outcomes obtain. "How possible" studies analyze the way some solutions and policies become seen as viable and necessary and others are excluded, based on how problems are constructed, who has the power to promote their constructions, and what techniques of power they use to promote, reinforce, and naturalize them (Doty 1996). Studying how security, threat, and otherness are constructed can excavate the problematic turning points and processes by which they become dominant, and critical theorists intend for this exposure to reduce their power, opening the way for a debate about alternatives.

Securitization Theory and New Conceptual Innovations in Security Studies

A final interpretivist approach to security examined in this chapter is the "securitization" or "Copenhagen School" developed in the early 1990s by Ole Wæver, Barry Buzan, and Jaap de Wilde. Beginning from the assertion that "security" itself is a fluid concept, securitization theorists are concerned with how and why political and social practices and issue-areas that are seemingly outside the mold of conventional security concerns become constituted as "existential threats" to valued "referent objects" (Buzan, Wæver, and de Wilde 1998; Hansen 2006: 35). How and why, in other words, do people, states, issues, movements, or identities become securitized, and is it possible (or desirable) to "desecuritize" them? Securitization, in this approach, is a *discursive* process, in which a threat is constructed as existential and in need of "extraordinary" and immediate measures to address it. This process, in turn, validates and legitimizes moves that go beyond "the established rules of the game" and "above politics" (Buzan, Wæver, and de Wilde 1998: 23).

To address these issues, we must again return to the concept of discourse and the rejection of the fact/value distinction. As Hansen points out, "For problems or facts to become questions of security, they need . . . to be successfully constructed as such within political discourse" (Hansen 2006: 33–34). This is accomplished through the performative use of language, usually by elites in authoritative positions, such as naming particular countries or groups as existential threats to a state or population's security or existence, putting such assertions into an intersubjectively understood context, and dramatizing an issue and presenting it "as an issue of supreme priority; thus, by labeling it as *security* an agent claims a need for and a right to treat it by extraordinary means" (Buzan, Wæver, and de Wilde 1998: 26, quoted in Peoples and Vaughan-Williams 2010: 78). Extraordinary means might include controlling information, the reduction or elimination of civil liberties, or the control of people's movements, among other possibilities. The inference is that the consequences of *not* taking such means would be "fatal" for the state and/or its population (Buzan 1998). Once again, there is no *a priori* definition of security; rather, it is a "political practice" with specific meanings that need to be understood and analyzed (Wæver 1995; Kurowska and Kratochwil 2012).

The concept of *national* security, then, invokes a necessary connection to the state and state sovereignty, "not because the state is an immortal entity or because security is objectively provided by the state, but because 'the meaning of security is tied to historically specific forms of political community'" (Walker 1990: 5, quoted in Hansen 2006: 34). Since the advent of modernity in Europe, this form has been dominated by the state, resulting in a rigid binary between the "domestic" and the "international" realms of order. "The national and the international are thus not simply two different political spheres but are constructed as each other's opposites, as each other's constitutive Other" (Hansen 2006: 34). Conventional security studies takes this binary as a given, using it as the foundation for determining which "Others" are the greatest threats to security and survival. As a result, securitization theorists as well as other critical security scholars in IR argue that this binary must be deconstructed in order to explicate the meanings behind concepts of threat, national interest, and the need for protection.

One of the major insights of securitization theory is the expansion of security logics to new areas of social and political life. Recent work by Mona Sheikh (2011), for example, noted in Chapter 5, explores the linkages between religion and security that dominate much debate in contemporary IR. Here again, by securitizing "religion," some conventional security studies create binaries between "religion" and "secularism," or "the West" and "Islam" (this is especially evident in Huntington 1996). Securitization scholars highlight the need for interpretivist research to uncover and expose the discursive processes by which such issues become securitized, asking whether and how it is possible to "de-securitize" them by changing the performative language that constructs them in terms of danger and threat.

New Directions in Interpretive International Security Studies

The concept of "ontological security" has been gaining ground as an important intervention in international security studies, and examines what might be called the opposite of securitization (Mitzen 2006; Steele 2008). The central puzzle addressed by this work concerns how and why states act in ways that do not appear to enhance their security interests in traditional terms (as in the case of Belgium in 1914), or act in ways that display unwillingness to escape danger and conflict (Mitzen 2006). Using insights from social psychology as well as the work of Alexander Wendt and Anthony Giddens, some scholars locate an important answer in states' "ontological security, or security of the self" (Mitzen 2006). Ontological security, then, focuses on states' conceptions of self, or self-identity. The concept of shame can function as a spur or a check on state actions, compelling it to act in some cases to preserve a sense of self that would otherwise be severely damaged (Steele 2008). This type of self-identity preservation, then, constitutes the "ontological security" that states go to great lengths to protect. Instead of the realist dictum that states behave in ways that enhance their material security interests, or the liberal assumption that states in the post-Cold war era are acting to foster new humanitarian and cosmopolitan norms, Steele (2008), for example, examines so-called "humanitarian" interventions, and argues that states engage in humanitarian actions not to foster cosmopolitan morality but rather to shore up their self-identities when they are shamed or otherwise threatened.

This concept still implies, however, that we can speak of such things as the "state" and its identity, which many critical theorists and feminists find particularly problematic. Kurowska and Tallis (2013) take a very different direction in rejecting any notion of state interests. Instead, they focus on pushing reflexivity in new directions. They do so ostensibly by analyzing security at the Polish-Ukrainian border, but this attempt quickly becomes an ever-deepening reflection on their own "normative dilemma of writing security" (Huysmans 2002), referring to how scholars inevitably mobilize and reproduce constructions, or "imaginaries," of the meaning of security. Kurowska, the scholar, returns to her hometown to do research on the meaning of security, and Tallis, the border guard "practitioner" of security, show in their writing their joint struggle to delineate the conditions of knowledge production of which they are part, and how they learn each other's security language while shedding and constantly questioning their presuppositions, both old and newly realized. Their reflexive sensibilities are both individual and mutual, and their object becomes less to discover any meanings for European security itself than to investigate the emotions generated in the construction of knowledge claims (on emotion see also Bially-Mattern 2011). In the process, they increasingly interrogate the meaning of their attempt to give up scholarly and professional authority and autonomy in favor of their ongoing reflexive engagement regarding knowledge construction (Kurowska and Tallis 2013). This engagement is ultimately a never-ending hermeneutical process that takes us ever deeper into the discursively mediated meanings of the concept of security itself.

Interpretive Contributions to International Security

Early interpretive works in international security include the classical realists as well as some of their opponents. Their writings do not self-consciously use the term "interpretivist," although they did follow a number of interpretivist tenets. They clearly articulate the need to situate their analyses in historical, social economic and political context, argue in favor of the constitutive nature of power and morality, and view both power and politics as fluid and in need of constant re-evaluation. The work of feminist theorists also reflect these tenets, but incorporates in addition a strongly reflexive stance vis-à-vis the relationship between gender and power. Feminists and critical theorists discuss more explicitly the interpretivist bases of their methodologies, including employing the concept of discourse to understand how threats are constructed and how the constitutive relationship between language and material forms of power gives meaning to who or what should be secure. All of these interpretivist security studies use their resulting conceptual frameworks and empirical studies to critique neorealism. The securitization literature adds an explicit focus on the meaning of security by emphasizing the process by which something becomes essential or "sacred" to it. This literature opens new ways to conceptualize the fluidity of meaning in the central focus of the subfield itself. Some recent work, finally, both returns to the state to work out a conceptualization of "ontological security" that both strengthens the focus on the state while paradoxically weakening its essentialist connotations, while other work pushes reflexivity in new directions in inserting the researcher and research subject into direct dialogue and mutual introspection in the research process.

The tight constitutive relationship among discourse and ethics underpins interpretive work on security. Perhaps because of the discursive and disciplinary power of various forms of realism, the goals of interpretive security studies tend to be those of critique and deconstruction rather than emancipation. Classical realists, along with some scholars of Wittgensteinian language games, prioritize *Verstehen* as a means of understanding "what is possible," while feminists and critical theorists deconstruct and critique conventional security assumptions, concepts, and findings. Some feminists, perhaps, go furthest towards emancipatory goals, but the recognition of the power of conventional security meanings and practices may militate against the belief that alternatives, if articulated, can change deeply engrained discursive patterns.

Notes

1   I say "at least partially" because there was little explicit consideration of race and virtually none of gender.
2   Perhaps even more interesting, scholars are now recovering the strongly historicized interest in global reform that characterized much classical realist thought but frequently escaped the analyses of neo-realist and critical scholars alike (see Scheurmann 2010).
3   Two exceptions are Simon Dalby's 1997 "Contesting an Essential Concept: Reading the Dilemmas in Contemporary Security Discourse," and Ken Booth's 1997 "Security and Self: Reflections of a Fallen Realist," both in Keith Krause & Michael C. Williams (eds), *Critical Security Studies,* Minneapolis: University of Minnesota Press.

3
INTERPRETING INTERNATIONAL POLITICAL ECONOMY

How is the global economy discursively constructed and ordered, and what are its political implications?

What is the relationship between theory and praxis in significant turning points in economic history?

How do gender, class, and race shape the global economy, and vice versa?

If interpretivist security studies focused on denaturalizing the constitutive nature of Cold War realism and strategic studies in international relations, interpretivist studies of international political economy (IPE) fulfill a similar role for liberalism, its precursors, and its heirs. Just as conventional security studies accord with realism's goal of maintaining international political order, conventional IPE accords with liberalism's goal of achieving prosperity through rational, self-interested, and individualistic behavior. "Traditional" IPE analyzes the interrelationship between wealth and power, or global economic processes and domestic ones, or connects global economic institutions and processes to bilateral, transnational, regional, or other cross-border issues, or examines historical and policy trends that connect the global economy to international security.

This chapter focuses on work that denaturalizes the methods, goals, and teleology of liberal scholarship. It therefore begins with Marx, whose corpus of work effectively exposed the symbiotic relationship between liberalism and capitalism obtaining in the mid-nineteenth century, although not out of interpretivist commitments or goals. Denaturalizing liberalism, however, also entails disentangling many of its component parts, from assumptions of rationalism (and later rational actor models) regarding how people act in economic "lifeworlds" (this term is taken from Jürgen Habermas to indicate the intersubjective or shared "horizon of . . . unproblematic beliefs": Habermas 1996: 22; 1990b: 135–136; see also

Crawford 2009: 188), to techniques and rules of trade, finance, and investment, to the interconnections between either mercantilism or liberalism and militarism. Interpretivist international political economy also looks at the relationship between global economies and "everyday" ones based on lived experiences. Feminist work has once again blazed the trail in examining the consequences and implications of global economic processes as well as the categories used to analyze them on gendered practices and outcomes, including the increasing responsibilities of women as both tenders of the hearth and workers who sell their labor, the power relations involved in male joblessness and the feminization of poverty, and changes in local governance and family structures.

Implicit in the previous chapter is the acknowledgement that interpretivists may emphasize security or economic questions in any given analysis, but they also frequently note their interrelationship (Peterson 2003; Enloe 1989/2000; Gill 1993; Ruggie 1998; True 2012). Thus the divisions between security, political economy, and also law and organization are of necessity arbitrary. This is the case as well for non-interpretivist analyses, but given that one of the goals of interpretivism is to understand how context shapes both our questions and our evidence, it becomes even more difficult to treat security or law and economics as discrete issue-areas. The discussion that follows reflects this complexity, while also demonstrating many of the insights that interpretivist IPE scholars have brought to the subfield.

The chapter analyzes how interpretive IR theory has incorporated insights from Karl Marx and Antonio Gramsci to Michel Foucault and beyond, including feminist and postcolonial scholars such as Chandra Mohanty and Gayatri Spivak. One of the central questions this chapter addresses is whether and how it is possible to move beyond liberalism and more recently neoliberalism in the current era of economic globalization, and if so, how and towards what. Critical IPE scholars who are also interpretivists draw on Marx but lean more towards Gramsci, because of the latter's more explicit incorporation of culture into understandings of power and hegemony. They also incorporate concepts articulated by Michel Foucault. Governmentality, for example, is helpful to many interpretivist IPE scholars who are centrally concerned with how power operates in the relationship between global and local political economies. And it is impossible to evaluate global economic relations between core and periphery, North and South, or East and West without taking on board postcolonial and feminist interpretive scholarship.

This chapter weaves interpretive IPE's conceptual contributions together with work on major historical transitions in the global economy and global/local issues of gender and power. For example, both Marx and Foucault were centrally concerned with the transition from feudalism to capitalism; from the Middle Ages to modernity. Karl Marx's analyses of this transition, the conditions of possibility of capitalism, and the role of class conflict continue to inspire interpretivist IPE scholars to probe the assumptions, power, and mechanics of modern (both post-feudal and contemporary) liberalism. The implications of this transition are also important for explicating subsequent transitions in global political economy, including changes in techniques of power and their internal contradictions. This chapter, therefore, addresses work on the medieval/feudal to modern/liberal transition, the change from British hegemony in the nineteenth century to U.S. hegemony in the twentieth, the transition from colonialism to postcolonialism, and the evolution from liberalism to neoliberalism. Conceptually, the chapter weaves into this chronology how interpretive research in IPE draws on the insights of interpretivism articulated in Chapter 1, and probes the tensions among analyses that aim to denaturalize, explicate, and emancipate. Finally, the chapter addresses newer themes that work backward as well as forward in history to reinterpret significant changes in global political economy, including the role of the Rhineland in the development of the European Union and the examination and contextualization of significant thinkers from the Scottish Enlightenment to the present.

Marx, Gramsci, and Power/Knowledge in Historical Transitions

In the 1970s and 1980s, most scholars demarcated IPE into three theoretical types: realism, liberalism, and Marxism. Marxist and neo-Marxist IPE scholars abounded during this period, which paralleled decolonization, the development of the Organization of Petroleum Exporting Countries (OPEC) in 1960, and the subsequent heyday of "Third World" activism in the international economic order. The "postcolony" (Mbembe 2001) challenged the built-in advantages of the powers of the Global North through the New International Economic Order (NIEO), with the support of analyses asserting that the structural and ever-deepening inequalities resulted from global trade, finance, and investment practices. While influential for several years, this attempt to reconfigure the knowledge/practice relationship in IPE so as to enact alternatives to market liberalism did not ultimately succeed, of course. Moreover, the numbers of self-described neo-Marxist IPE theorists have declined since that time, a phenomenon that can be traced to the interpretivist insight that the sociology and historiography of knowledge construction is intimately bound up with power relations. By the 1990s, discursive conventions changed, and Marxism dropped out of the theoretical troika, a casualty of the end of the Cold War for the largely Western IR academy despite its continued resonance in many other parts of the world. It was replaced by constructivism, which itself had liberal as well as more critical variants (Klotz and Lynch 2007). Because interpretivist IPE, however, builds on even while it differs from the analyses of economic power developed by Marx and Engels, it is necessary to begin with a brief overview of the insights which have shaped interpretive work in the subfield.

Marx and Engels analyzed the mechanisms by which feudalism declined, especially the way in which the growth of new forms of local and global capital commodified labor, and how the development of property rights became progressively disentangled from the land-owning nobility while also producing new forms of alienation and poverty. As Justin Rosenberg insists, perhaps the primary result of this transition, which began with the political transformation from Empire to Absolute Monarchy, was the creation of a "private," productive sphere that includes a civil society that is abstracted from the "state-political sphere." Whereas the state developed discrete political boundaries, relations of production and exchange were allowed and encouraged to cross borders.

The sovereign state and "privatized" capitalism created what Rosenberg calls a new form of empire—"the empire of civil society"—which transnationalized production on the part of economic actors who appear to be independent from "politics" (by forming "civil society"), although in practice they depend on the state's agreement and support (Rosenberg 1994).

Thus far, this analysis is not particularly interpretivist, because it assumes the reality of a world "out there" that simply needs to be exposed and is only tangentially dependent on discursive tendencies. But there is also always lurking in Marxist analysis a trenchant critique of the construction of knowledge and power. Robert W. Cox and later Stephen Gill, among others, appealed to insights from Antonio Gramsci, the Italian communist who, while imprisoned by Benito Mussolini in the 1920s, wrote in *The Prison Notebooks* that the ideological and cultural bases of capitalism and liberalism reinforced and strengthened not only material inequalities but also ideological buy-in on the part of large sections of the populace (Gramsci 1971/1999). Gramsci's work provided a way to understand both the strength and character of global economic hegemony and the apparent consent of those who lost out because of it. Gramscians in IPE, then, provide an analysis of global economic inequalities that is constitutive of materialist *and* ideational factors. Still, there is variation regarding the degree to which Gramscians in IR can be seen as interpretivists, as discussed below.

Cox's classic article on "Social forces, states, and world orders: beyond international relations theory" (1981) was also one of the earliest pieces to adopt a largely interpretivist stance on the construction of knowledge in IR. He argued that theoretical starting points were merely "academic conventions" that represent a "cutting up of reality" in ways that are "just a convenience of the mind" (Cox 1996: 85). This article also includes his famous and oft-repeated dictum: "theory is always *for* someone and *for* some purpose" (Cox 1996: 87—see also Chapter 1 of this volume), indicating the necessity of always looking at the relations of power and production embodied in efforts to advance knowledge. In particular, Cox advocated *critical* rather than "problem-solving" theory, because the former was "dedicated to the social and political complex as a whole rather than to the separate parts. . . . whereas the problem-solving approach leads to further analytical subdivision and limitation of the issue to be dealt with, the critical approach leads toward the construction of a larger picture of the whole" (Cox 1996: 89). Problem-solving theory epitomized liberal IPE, which focused on how to increase cooperation among states in the belief that better order, efficiency, and prosperity would result. Critical theory, for Cox, was emancipatory, although it, too, could not escape the hermeneutic circle: "the more sophisticated a theory is, the more it reflects upon and transcends its own perspective; but the initial perspective is always contained within a theory and is relevant to its explication. There is, accordingly, no such thing as theory in itself, divorced from a standpoint in time and space" (Cox 1996: 87–88). Liberal theory needed to acknowledge that its concerns and frameworks were constitutive of the hegemonic post-World War II political-economic order, and that it played a role in reinforcing that order by its own intellectual production.

Cox's challenge to the fact/value distinction relies in particular on Gramsci's conceptualization of hegemony, which has a strong cultural and ideational as well as material basis. Cox notes that structural approaches to knowledge in both Marxism and realism took off in the 1960s, an era in which the liberal world economy and the superpower rivalry appeared increasingly settled and therefore permanent. Thus he shows that knowledge formation is conditioned by historical circumstances, and that allegedly objective theorizing is crafted in ahistorical terms but is still embedded in particular contexts of power, with particular policy goals. Truth is contextual and always fleeting, and "real history" refers more to the effects of economic power relations on lived experience than any positivist notion of "reality."

As a result, it is necessary to examine knowledge/practice constructs to evaluate both economic institutions and theories of international political economy. Institutions, for example, "reflect the power relations prevailing at their point of origin and . . . encourage collective images consistent with these power relations." This is what enables hegemony, such that relations of production, or economic relations, shape social forces in ways that support dominant (or hegemonic) power (Cox 1996: 99). Neorealist and liberal internationalist (and later neoliberal) theory, therefore, fulfills "a proselytizing function" for these forms of economic power, in naturalizing specific forms of rationality by treating them as simply the way states and economic "man" operate (Cox 1996: 93).

Global hegemonies that have been of primary concern to IPE scholars include the nineteenth-century *pax Britannica* and the post-World War II *pax Americana,* in which each successive hegemon was able to set up international financial, investment, and trade "rules of the game" to coalesce and reinforce its power. They did so insisting that their rules—and the institutions they spearheaded—were critically necessary for the good of the system, and that others in the system needed to coalesce around these institutions. The ability to shape what appears to be legitimate and necessary demonstrates how the diffusion of cultural norms is indispensable for hegemons to consolidate institutional power.

As a result, interpretivist IPE scholars probe the reasons for and modalities of a second major temporal marker: the transfer of hegemony from Great Britain to the United States. For interpretivists, a major question concerns whether there were qualitative differences in the meaning of these two hegemonic orders, and if so, what were they and what were their implications? John Ruggie's work on "embedded liberalism" (1982), drawing from that of Karl Polanyi (1944), addresses these issues. Like Cox, Ruggie does so in order to understand the meaning of the relationship between economic power and "social purpose" and their implications for global order.

While there are significant differences between the two authors (discussed below), Ruggie, like Cox, is interested in the "social purpose" that the intersection between international and domestic authority produces. Ruggie asks a Weberian question regarding the "economic ethic" of the *pax Britannica* vis-à-vis the *pax Americana,* although he does not employ the term. Ruggie's work inspired much of the early 1980s literature on "international regimes," the idea that issue-areas such as trade, money, and investment (as well as non-economic issue-areas) were ordered and governed by the "Great Powers" in specific ways. To understand international political economy, we needed to look not only at discrete state behavior but also at the principles, norms, rules, and procedures of this ordering (see also the discussion of Kratochwil and Ruggie 1986 in the next chapter).

The move from British to U.S. economic hegemony, like the relationship between state and empire, once again highlights the intimate relationships between military and political power, on the one hand, and economic power on the other. More specifically, the insights of Karl Polanyi and Charles Kindleberger expose the dual logics at play in security versus political economy: the former is supposed to be led by state interests, while the latter is allegedly regulated by the "invisible hand" of economic liberalism, as articulated by Adam Smith.

Yet, as Polanyi (1944/57) argues, nineteenth-century international economic policy, founded on the gold standard and principles of *laissez-faire* in trade, were in fact conceptualized and directed *by the state* across Europe, and this was especially the case in Britain. Ruggie emphasizes that, in Polanyi's words, "Laissez-faire was planned," and the development of the nineteenth-century market economy relied on the "strong state" to push forward the social transformations it required (Polanyi 1944/57: 141, quoted in Ruggie, 1998: 67).

When the social dislocations, market crash, and skyrocketing unemployment in the aftermath of the First World War shook the foundations of *laissez-faire* liberalism, state governments attempted to continue as before, leading to the infamous "beggar-thy-neighbor" policies that destroyed international economic cooperation in favor of short-term self-interested behavior. But these policies only produced a greater economic crisis, eventually delegitimizing British leadership of the world economy. Ruggie points out that the new order that was planned at the wartime Bretton Woods conference in 1944 represented a direct reaction on the part of U.S. and British authorities to interwar domestic problems. The new postwar regime, which he calls "embedded liberalism," was promoted by the United States at Bretton Woods to allow a certain amount of flexibility in trade and monetary relations among states, in order to enable them to regulate financial flows, protect some areas of trade, and ensure a basic level of employment. Liberalism continued to rule, but it was tamed and reframed in order to accord with states' "social purpose" (Ruggie 1998: 72–73).

Thus we have a better understanding of the meaning of hegemony and the reasons for differences over time. Late nineteenth century British hegemony relied on financial stability through the gold standard and massive investment (or, rather, massive colonialism) abroad;[1] U.S. hegemony relied on managing post-World War II growth and stability, especially on the part of Europe, Japan, and North America, through trade and monetary relations as well as alliance systems that took some account of domestic economic needs. Ruggie again emphasizes the interpretivist argument that focusing merely on "material" power relations or balances of power cannot explain the qualitative difference between hegemonic orders; instead, the authority relations reflecting social purpose also need to be analyzed. As a corollary, issue-areas such as international trade and monetary relations display complex relations of authority and power that cross and complicate the allegedly firm "inside/outside" boundaries of state sovereignty (on the "inside/outside" problematique, see Walker 1993; for a more state-centric view, see Helleiner 1994).

The approaches of Cox and Ruggie represent two significant strands of interpretivist IPE work: Gramscian and critical liberal perspectives. They display different goals—emancipation through critique versus *Verstehen* through explication (see Chapter 1)—and hence different stances toward economic hegemony. These goals need not be mutually exclusive, but authors such as Cox and Ruggie tend to emphasize one over the other. Both approaches, however, reject the reduction of international economic relations to economic indices of power. Both are interpretive though they represent different interpretivist goals, and both react to major innovations in the global economy from before the Second World War through the 1970s, when successive oil crises, the debacle of the Vietnam War, and the creation of the Organization of the Petroleum Exporting Countries (OPEC) caused academics and policy-makers in liberal powers to question whether their relative power, especially their relative economic power, was in decline (see especially Keohane and Nye 1977). This overarching question prompted further inquiries, for example, whether issues such as floating exchange rates, moves to protect or liberalize trade sectors, and changes in investment flows represented major transformations that needed to be analyzed as such, or were ways of working through the kinks in the global economic order that were of minor long-term significance given the overarching power of liberal capitalism. Many interpretivists thought the latter in the 1970s and early 1980s, but the advent of what became known as "neoliberalism" in the late 1980s and 1990s brought these questions again to the forefront.[2]

Both Ruggie and Cox focused on the endurance of international institutions constitutive of liberal capitalism but left room open for analytical and substantive possibilities for change. Cox, especially, linked change to the need for critical analysis and reflexivity on the part of theorists who participate in knowledge construction. Others who analyzed the stability of post-World War II liberal capitalism from a neo-Marxist or Gramscian point of view tended to focus on its stability and power, even while they deplored its uneven and deleterious effects. Susan Strange, for example, also critiqued theory in articulating "the famous four structures of international political economy—production, finance, security and the knowledge structure." Strange demonstrated both "a deep sense of injustice and corruption" with how "business conducts its affairs, which she disliked with passion," and also "a deep sense of frustration with academia ... which she considered to be supportive either directly, or indirectly, of American hegemony by diverting attention from the real issues facing the world" (Palan 2003: 121, 133; see also Strange 1986, 1987, and 1996). Despite her inclusion of knowledge as a "structure," however, Strange remained rooted in a very materialist understanding of political economy, as opposed to the more interpretivist insights opened up by Cox's framework of analysis. For the former, scholars' willful limitations are a significant problem for understanding how the world works; for the latter, knowledge production by problem-solving scholars is a constitutive feature of economic and political power.

Feminist International Political Economy

If we open the boundaries of Cox's "social and political complex" or Strange's "four structures of international political economy" to explicate significant practices and processes of international political economy, how far should we go? What matters besides whether monetary rates are fixed or flexible, or to what degree trade is protected or "free," or how crony capitalism operates, or how knowledge production supports liberal hegemonies? Feminist IPE scholars, who overlap with their security counterparts, reformulate these questions in insisting that everyday economies are intimately tied to transnational ones, and that the constitutive nature of family and market on both local and transnational levels means that we need to investigate once again the gendered nature of international economic practices in our research. It is not merely, then, "domestic social purpose" that matters, but more important are the local and transnational ways that social purpose and practice play out for women and men, families and other systems of organization and authority. The feminization of poverty is no accident, but is directly related to institutions and social purposes that are woven into the fabric of IPE.

In addition to the physical violence that militarized institutions perpetuate vis-à-vis women (see Chapter 2), local and transnational economic institutions promote the gendered nature of labor, trade, finance, investment, and technology. The Gramscian approach discussed above retains class as a major factor of analysis and criticizes the devaluing of labor, especially in "developing" countries. Feminists, however, highlight how the worlds of finance, investment and technology are gendered, ruled by hegemonic masculinities that suppress or subordinate other forms of masculinity as well as femininity, excluding women in the process. These insights, according to feminists, are still insufficiently incorporated into many critical analyses.

Again, feminist theorists show that, in order to understand and explicate gendered divisions of labor locally and globally, we cannot merely employ an inductive method of "adding and stirring" women into the mix. At the most basic level, scholars need to look at the constitutive relationship between gendered labor and gendered discursive constructions. The resulting

> gender stereotypes . . . are promulgated by dualistic categories favored in economic analysis: paid-unpaid work, production-reproduction, skilled-unskilled, formal-informal. These interact with other gendered dichotomies that shape how we think about work: 'men's work'—'women's work,' labor for profit-labor for love, working-caretaking, breadwinner-housewife, and family wage earner-'pin money' wage earner.
>
> *(Peterson and Runyan 1999: 130)*

Many feminist theorists point out that women's work is often not counted or valued because it is "informal" and frequently considered to be "private." Public/private distinctions in both liberal economic theory and state (and inter-state) practice are not objective facts but instead are constructed—yet powerful—discursive strategies. Their influence on knowledge production, which takes the public/private categories and the marginalization of "women's work" for granted, creates and continues to worsen the feminization of poverty. Informal, "private" work includes, in addition to the sex industry, a wide variety of home-based forms of labor, including child-rearing (one's own children or the children of others), maid services, and "'petty' trading of mostly small, inexpensive commodities ranging from vegetables to handicrafts and subcontracted, home-based piecework" (Peterson and Runyan 1999: 141).

Peterson and Runyan analyze earlier research in feminist IPE to point out that home-based work is usually thought to be a component of the industrial revolution that has been superseded by a more thorough institutionalization of the commodification and valuation of labor. They argue, however, that it is instead increasing, due to corporate strategies to outsource or subcontract production and the need for women to supplement family incomes (Peterson and Runyan 1999: 141). The results include sweatshops and indentured servitude, in the Global North as well as the Global South, the impoverishment of feminized global labor, and an intimate relationship between gendered global economic processes and the militarized state (Enloe 1989/2000).

In order to expose, understand and explicate the gendered implications of market practices, feminist theorists have "denaturalized the rules of the market" (Prügl 1998: 135), demonstrating first, that the vast amount of informal and marginalized work is done primarily by women, and second, that this informal work is not simply a product of women's entrepreneurial strategies in the face of poverty or limited opportunities. Instead, the opportunities women are able to create are intimately tied to state policies and globalized norms and practices.

As Prügl points out, "The gendered roles of households, labor markets, and states powerfully conspire to effect a construction of home-based work as secondary," resulting in "very different meanings in different contexts" (Prügl 1998: 130–131; see also Whitworth 1994). For Prügl, the relationship between rules and meaning is primary. "Labor market practices reinforce rules that construct home-based workers as nonworkers and their work as secondary and subordinate." Moreover, rules underpin and reinforce laws which not only make women's work invisible but also deny them workers' rights. "Most perniciously, these rules legitimate the puny wages of home-based workers" (Prügl 1998: 135).

The feminization of poverty, then, is not merely a matter of lack of economic opportunity or even sexism in the home, although these can both be important factors. Rather, the very workplace norms instituted by labor also devalue work done primarily by women, and women's rights are denied by the relative lack of organizing and political support compared, for example, to successful unionization strategies in sectors dominated by male workers. Peterson and Runyan agree, returning to the transition from feudalism to capitalism to explicate the gendered division of labor globally in the liberal economic order:

> European state-making, the growth of capitalism, and subsequent Western colonization must be understood as interactive processes. They tend to overlap in institutionalizing more rigid, less equal, and, thus, less complementary conceptions of how labor should be divided between the sexes, between classes, and between nations. . . . the division of women's and men's work is rooted firmly in patriarchal conceptions of women's and men's 'nature' that are inextricable from a liberal-capitalist model of state-based society.
>
> *(Peterson and Runyan 1999: 131)*

Many types of traditionally "women's work," moreover, are produced by the confluence of global economic and military processes. Cynthia Enloe and Jan Jindy Pettman have shown how prostitution is constitutive of gendered divisions of labor and gendered practices of militarism, which Pettman calls "'the international political economy of sex'" (Pettman 1996: 197–198; Enloe 1989/2000; Peterson and Runyan 1999: 138). Women who become vulnerable to sex tourism and trafficking as well as military base prostitution frequently have few options, in part because both the tourist and military industries frequently displace local economic practices and control of property. Instead of women participating in local systems of production and control, their bodies become central objects in the revamped political economies of security and tourism.

These forms of critical (Enloe, Peterson, and Runyan) and constructivist (Prügl) feminist IPE are interpretive because they rely on insights regarding the significance of discursive forms of power (ones based on linguistic binary constructions but extending to relations and sites of production and law) to investigate the gendered nature of global economic relations and their localized manifestations.

V. Spike Peterson sums up the central insights of critical feminist IPE by arguing that the globalization of capitalism and the accompanying spread of consumerism relies on three "mutually constituted" kinds of economies: the reproductive, the productive, and the virtual, or "RPV" (Peterson 2003). Specifically, the market subsumes the "reproductive economy," penetrating

> the most intimate spheres of social life. Activities previously considered non-waged and private—sexual relations, biological and social reproduction, leisure activities, household maintenance—are increasingly commodified and drawn into circuits of capital accumulation. Infants, human organs, sexualized bodies, intimate caring, sensual pleasures, and spiritual salvation are all for sale.
> *(Peterson 2003: 78)*

Feminists have long criticized the boundaries between "public" work that is remunerated versus "private" work that is not, but Peterson goes a significant step further in articulating gendered reproductive politics as its own "economy," albeit one that is constituted alongside the more conventional "productive" economy and the ever-changing "virtual" one of information, financial, and symbolic flows. While not isolating gender within the reproductive economy, this framework at the same time clarifies how logics and discourses of reproduction that depend on women's bodies intersect with forms of production and economic circulation (financial transactions, for example), that appear at first glance to have little to do with women's interests or participation. Peterson argues that her "critical rewriting of global political economy" makes sense of, and thereby politicizes, financial, virtual, and gendered labor trends in global politics.

Peterson's method in this later work is more explicitly interpretivist in its attention to discourse and method, because it advances a "relational framing" of these economies "that posits identities (subjectivity, self-formation), meaning systems (symbols, discourse, ideologies), and social practices/institutions (actions/social structures) as *co-constituting* dimensions of social reality" (Peterson 2003: 1, 40). She takes as a starting point the approach articulated by Ferdinand de Saussure (see Chapter 1), which reformulates the linguistic challenge to the fact/value distinction by asserting that there is an arbitrary relationship between the "signifier" (word or symbol) and the "signified" (the object or entity being described or symbolized). Yet the *process* of signification tends to stabilize and give power to some meanings over others. As Derrida pointed out in his articulation of "difference," significations accrue power because they are developed in opposition to other ones deemed less worthy. The meanings and relationships that result are not absolute, but they do elevate and make possible some forms of knowledge and frameworks of understanding while discounting others (Peterson 2003: 42).

Peterson's volume represented part of a new round of feminist interpretive IPE work, which also began to bring in more nuanced and complex understandings of women's agency vis-à-vis globalizing market forces, rather than viewing women as relatively passive subjects of power/knowledge relationships. Jacqui

True, for example, explored the dual nature of Czech women's agency and positionality following the end of the Cold War, when liberalization after the fall of communism in the Czech Republic resulted in the imposition of market institutions and logics (True 2003). While Enloe and others looked at gendered IPE in a sense from the "top down," True demonstrates "how the globalization process might be rethought from the 'bottom-up', in terms of changes in social relations upon which other, more macro changes are sustained" (True 2003: 163).

True finds that post-Cold War globalization, and Czech women's responses to it, simultaneously produce inequality, objectification and empowerment, outcomes that are not necessarily seen to coexist easily. One (typical) effect has been an increase in women's work at home. "By redistributing resources in a self-sacrificing way and doing more, not less, work in the home, women have often cushioned the transition" from socialism to capitalism, taking on the burden and reducing the shock of the transition to other actors (True 2003: 111). Yet other aspects of capitalism have had mixed effects. For example, Western marketing campaigns targeted to increase women's consumption of beauty products have proven very popular, adding to women's objectification and gender differentiation while simultaneously enhancing women's power as consumers. Finally, women's activism in organizing against sexual abuse and discrimination has risen, frequently supported by the very multinational entities, including *Harlequin* and *Cosmopolitan,* that strive to create gender difference based on bodily appearances (True 2003: 117).

True's work, while forming part of a second generation of feminist IR/IPE, also contributes to a more generalized move in IPE to understand the complicated effects of the mutual constitution of culture and production. These include, for example, the "limits to liberalization" in the production and protection of local and national cultures in the "global marketplace" (Goff 2007), and, conversely, the relationship between American cultural production and warfare in the globalization of "Hollyworld" (Hosic 2002). These works provide a cautionary note regarding the emancipatory goals of critical interpretivist work, suggesting instead that the intersection of political economy and cultural production, or the discursively constructed nexus of knowledge and power, are unstable and in need of constant assessment and reflexivity.

Feminist and Postcolonial Approaches

Postcolonial insights also contribute to feminist IPE (and vice versa), by highlighting the particular burden in the global economy borne by women of color and women from the Global South. Increasingly, interpretivists are demonstrating additional implications of gendered forms of subjectivity and positionality. For example, because gender is a social construction that has ramifications for everyone, many feminists point out that it is a necessary lens through which to examine the problematic effects of gendered practices of political economy on men as well as women. While gendered economies rarely benefit women (although some argue that women did well in many non-Western, pre-modern forms of local political economy), their effects on men, especially minority men in the Global North and non-elite men in the Global South, are frequently deleterious, and can worsen the state of gender relations overall.

Men as well as women in the Global South, for example, became impoverished by the appropriation of land by colonizing powers. This phenomenon, justified by racialized legitimizations of "tutelage" and "civilizing missions" (see, for example, Doty 1996), robbed men of much of their livelihoods, such that they then became plantation workers employed in doing farmwork that had been the province of women, and being cast as both lazy and effeminate by colonial property owners as a result. As Gita Sen and Caren Grown observe, "The colonial period created and accentuated inequalities both 'among' nations, and between classes and genders (also castes, ethnic communities, races, etc.) 'within' nations" (Sen and Grown 1998, quoted in Peterson and Runyan 1999: 132). Similarly, Mrinalini Srinha points out that colonial systems created hierarchies of economic and political power, with men who were constructed as more feminized placed lower than those who were constructed as more masculinized (Srinha 1995).

Because of the critical emphasis on the inequalities produced by capitalism in conjunction with colonialism, many feminists and postcolonial analysts focus on the critical implications of creating liberal markets in non-Western socio-economic contexts (Spivak 1988, 1998; Mohanty 2003). They draw on but also complicate and challenge neo-Marxist "dependency" theory, which took off in 1970s Latin America in an era of growing Third World debt, impoverishment of populations, and elite perpetuation of violence. Dependency theory divided the world into a "core" where wealth, finance, and decision-making power were concentrated and a "periphery" from which resources were extracted and where local forms of production had been replaced by cash crops, mining, and other industries that would increase exports. Dependency and world systems theorists (who added a "semi-periphery" to the mix and added a much longer historical perspective) both asserted that the global economy was run from the core with the cooperation of elites from the periphery, and that as the core and these elites benefited from the exploitation of resources and labor in the periphery, the majority of the populace in the periphery became increasingly impoverished. Given international financial and debt flows, the liberal capitalist "solutions" to these inequities—increasing borrowing and decreasing social spending—only reinforced and worsened the structural inequalities caused by capitalism. Especially with the advent of "neo-liberalism" in the 1980s (as opposed to "embedded liberalism" that relied on state intervention to ensure domestic employment goals, neoliberal practices attempt to restrict the role of the state to policies that support market forces, with little if any attention to social dislocations—see Harvey 2005: 2), international financial institutions such as the International Monetary Fund and the World Bank imposed new austerity measures on "developing" states. Structural Adjustment Programmes (or SAPs), which require states to reduce spending on social programs, health, and education, and generally remove subsidies on necessary food items such as bread, sugar, and rice produced locally in order to open up borders to foreign products, became the norm for reducing state spending in order to increase debt payments and exports. The result, as dependency and world systems theorists, critical and postcolonial scholars and feminists agree, is frequently drastic for those already on the margins. Cynthia Enloe, for example, shows how, for example, politicians in indebted governments make gendered calculations about how much social dislocation populations will endure, how the costs can be shifted largely to women's work, and how remittance policies reinforce and promote the emigration of women from countries such as Sri Lanka and the Philippines to find work as domestics abroad (Enloe 1989/2000: 184–188).

Again, however, interpretivist approaches differ from those, such as dependency and world systems, that posit the existence of "objective" structures that derive from exclusively material relations of power. Nevertheless, many interpretivists or interpretivist-leaning scholars, including feminists such as Enloe, have drawn from this general framework while also examining the constitutive role of gender, culture and race in global economic practices. Historically, each of these frameworks emerged from a broader concern with the meaning and implications of market liberalism, particularly in relation to mercantilist policies that are supposedly the antithesis of *laissez-faire*. Interpretivist insights on colonialism carry a reminder that the "state" is not only a construction, but also a very imperfect description, at best, of the political entities that have been most powerful during the modern era. Virtually all of the "great powers" of the nineteenth and twentieth centuries can also be described as "empires," given their colonization of non-European areas of the world. (Despite the United States' self-identity as a critic of imperialism and proponent of freedom, interpretivists point out that its role in the Philippines, Hawaii, and Latin America enables it to fit easily into the category of imperial power as well (Doty 1996; Campbell 1992/1998)). This interpretivist critical and postcolonial scholarship asks whether and how mercantilism and empire survive in relations between what are known today as the "Global North" and the "Global South," despite pretensions to the egalitarianism that liberalism is supposed to foster, and what are the meanings and implications of their co-existence.

As a result, interpretivist IPE scholars have engaged with the analyses of Michel Foucault on the critical importance of examining discursive power in the transition from liberal to neoliberal practices. Foucault's corpus of work connected discursive microprocesses (including terminology, design/architecture/art, organizational management, specific technological innovations) to macrodevelopments such as the change from pre-modernity to modernity and more recently, from liberalism to neoliberalism, to demonstrate the mechanisms and techniques of liberal governance that produce and reproduce relations of power, and that create discursively produced boundaries between "public" and "private" in liberal modernity (Foucault 1997/1995; Burchell, Gordon and Miller, 1991; Rabinow 1984). Labeled "governmentality," this concept includes the Gramscian insight regarding the consent of the governed in relations of power, but deepens and extends this insight by incorporating the notion of consent into a detailed examination of the discursive processes and techniques that consolidate and normalize liberal governance.

Gramscian work in IPE, then, aligns with Foucauldian insights that assertions of truth can never be complete and always contain significant contradictions that can open the way to alternatives. For example, in previous work on the anti-globalization movement (Lynch 1998), I employed Gramsci to analyze the "discursive demobilization" that accompanies labor, environmental, feminist and peace movements' slow and partial responses to neoliberalism. In the 1980s and early 1990s, these movements remained ensconced in identity politics rather than challenging market forces, foregoing the opportunity to form the kind of "counter-hegemonic bloc" called for by Gramsci to expose hegemonic knowledge construction and material practices. Reversing their discursive demobilization required such an exposure, by confronting more directly the dismantling of state welfare policies in the name of market liberalization. I concluded that, despite the beginnings of the anti-globalization movement in the 1990s, such radical and widespread changes in discursive power would be difficult to achieve. Foucault, however, provides an additional insight: while contradictions can produce "ruptures" in political, economic and social practices, and while these can open the way to alternative forms of power, new configurations and techniques of power always contain new forms of domination. Thus, while there are similarities between the Gramscian/Cox concept of dialectic and the Foucauldian notion of contradictions that can produce discursive ruptures, the latter are both less intentional and more susceptible to fall far short of any emancipatory ideal. Nevertheless, critical IPE theorists sometimes employ insights from both Gramsci and Foucault (as well as from other social theorists including Louis Althusser and Stuart Hall) to explicate the constitutive power of political economic discourses (see, for example, Doty 1996 and Dunn 2003).

Feminist IPE scholars also take these concepts as a point of departure, but in employing the work of theorists like Gayatri Spivak, they also articulate the kinds of reflexivity that are necessary to break through the inevitably gendered forms of power and allow the possibility of emancipation. In a famous article, "Can the Subaltern Speak?" (1988), Spivak argues that women in the Global South are "subaltern" subjects who are treated by globalized systems of production and knowledge as "invisible," without their own history, experiences, or voices. She implicates both neoliberal forms of "empire" and the largely Western academy—both female and male—in creating a new type of gendered subaltern in the postcolonial era, one who is constructed by and caught in the "complicity between cultural and economic value systems" (Spivak 1987: 166, quoted in Peterson 2003: 1). What this means is that academics, and particularly Western feminists, frequently presume to "speak for" women in the Global South. As a result, Spivak, as Catarina Kinnvall points out, articulates an important critique of Western feminist privilege, and poses a central ethical challenge to the Western feminist academic: how to "unlearn" her "female privilege" and "learn to speak to (rather than listen to or speak for) the historically muted subject of the subaltern woman," in order "to prevent the continued construction of the subaltern" (Kinnvall 2009: 327). As Kinnvall further asserts, "Spivak's criticism of privileged academic intellectuals who claim to speak for the disenfranchised woman in the global South" has had a significant impact on critical feminist IR (Kinnvall 2009: 324). This is because she challenges interpretivist IPE scholars, both self-identified feminists and others, to engage in new forms of reflexivity that require transformed relationships with research subjects as well as potentially transformed research processes.

Feminists and critical scholars continue to struggle with the implications of Spivak's critique, as it strikes at the heart of interpretivist insights regarding the researcher's positionality vis-à-vis the hermeneutic circle and the constitutive relationship between power and knowledge construction (see, for example, Stern 2006; D'Costa 2006). Feminist IPE scholars increasingly seek not only to highlight the voices of marginalized and frequently impoverished populations, but also to reject victimhood in favor of demonstrating the discursive forms of power that produce and reproduce inequalities. Feminists also insist that researchers examine ways to shed our privileged positions in the global economy, calling us to be relentless in exchanging comfortable critiques for unsettling forms of interrogation, including of ourselves.

Recent Directions: Reinterpreting Enlightenment Thinkers and European Historical Processes

Recent work in IPE continues to expand its focus to finding new ways of conceptualizing forms of neoliberal governmentality in "developing" areas of the world and probing the relationship among cultural, political, and economic processes. In addition, however, some scholars are returning to the thinkers and sites of Europe to examine "classic" IPE theorists from the Scottish Enlightenment (Blaney and Inayatullah 2010) and the geographical space out of which European trade flourished and capitalism and the state were born (Loriaux 2008). Each of these trends rejects the notion of a separate "economic" sphere of life that modern economics tries to delineate and that Karl Polanyi criticized so well (Polanyi 1944/1957). Instead, as for Peterson and others, developments in productive capacities are understood as constitutive of social, political, cultural, and technological processes and practices.

As David Blaney and Naeem Inayatullah assert, returning to the Scottish Enlightenment (as well as nineteenth century modern German thinkers from Hegel to Marx) allows us to evaluate directly the moral purposes of capitalist production and market ideology. Scottish Enlightenment thinkers such as Adam Smith, James Steuart, and Adam Ferguson did not shy away from such introspection; rather it was part and parcel of their theoretical development. Indeed, according to Blaney and Inayatullah, all three "worried that *poverty might be intrinsic to wealth creation.*" As a result, they "believe that classical political economy's moral vibrancy results from how honestly they wrestled with this wound of wealth." This new reading of Smith and others, like challenges to the interpretations of neo-realist readings of Thucydides, Machiavelli, and Hobbes, can reveal "alternative ways of thinking about poverty (and wealth), about the character of modern civil or market society, and about the nature of historical progress itself" (Blaney and Inayatullah 2010: 2, 3). Like those who return to ancient or modern philosophy and classical realism, the point of this re-examination is to read these authors in their own historical context, breaking through "the defense of purity" of modern market economies to reveal their social costs and open up alternatives. Blaney and Inayatullah thus argue that attempting to understand the "concepts . . . distinctions, and . . . beliefs" of past thinkers aids in understanding "that our current values and visions, and the social practices they inform, cannot be taken for granted, but 'reflect a series of choices made at different times between different possible worlds.'" They characterize such a reading as "healing" the allegedly inherent conflict between "political and ethical discourse" (2010: 4, 6). Their work, along with that of others who traverse the boundaries of intellectual history and international relations, serves to highlight conceptual innovation by situating it temporally and contextually. This recovery of meaning of political concepts is interpretivist in that it attempts to open up methodological as well as ethical questions and debate.

Michael Loriaux also brings critical insights back to Europe in his richly detailed political economy of the "Rhineland frontier's" cultural geography (Loriaux 2008). He argues that "European Union is about deconstructing the Rhineland frontier," although this "fact" has been obfuscated by "ontopologies" (mythical constructions of the essence of places) that focus on Europe as a collection of nation-states (2008: 32). It is interesting, although not part of Loriaux's argument, that classical economic theory was born out of the consolidation of the state, and that its moral purpose was to soften if not erase state boundaries in favor of prosperity for all. This idealization of both state and market economy as necessary adversaries is also an "ontopology," a term that Loriaux borrows from Derrida. But Loriaux instead insists on demonstrating in detail the cultural as well as economic and political entity that comprises the Rhineland from the Roman era to the present European Union. Focusing on the Rhineland as the core pulsating commercial, developmental, industrial, and civilizational artery of Europe allows us to see its role as linchpin between the Baltic and North Seas and the Mediterranean, as the place where cities flourished (at ports, on rivers, in lowlands and mountains), where cultures intermingled, and where the nation-state was eventually superimposed, creating mythologies about otherness that persist to the present. Loriaux's analysis, also, once again, reveals the power of discourse to shape geopolitical imaginaries and delimit the EU's moral purpose. Instead, he offers a "vision of a *plurilingual* Greater Rhineland" that could be

> a place of encounter, of urban civilization, of cultural invention, of informal, networked governance. It becomes meaningful as a site that mobilizes and legitimates, not merely by recalling the pathologies of territorial closure in the past, but by recalling civilizational possibilities that one might *recon*-struct as suggestive, inspirational legacy.
>
> *(Loriaux 2008: 329–330)*

This construction of new meaning is, as he acknowledges, a "vision," but one that is grounded in the openings that past meanings could arguably make possible. Ultimately, Loriaux argues in favor of the possibilities of a new kind of cosmopolitanism, unlike most postcolonial theorists. This type of cosmopolitanism, however, would be one "that takes root in geographical fact, a cosmopolitanism that is not 'uprooted,' not imported." This is a regional cosmopolitanism, then, not a global one. To reimagine cosmopolitanism itself as a limited geographic enterprise is a bold move (and one that will be taken up in the subsequent chapter). But Loriaux's project also moves beyond the dichotomy between critique and emancipation to aspire to "discovery, invention, creation, and reconstruction" (Loriaux 2008: 329–330).

These interrogations of global and regional political economies highlight the relationship between power and knowledge and the need for intertextual investigation. They resonate with the insights of recent feminist and postcolonial theorists, moreover, in rejecting globalized forms of power and knowledge that mask the experiences and histories of different populations, localities, and regions.

Interpretive Contributions to International Political Economy

Much interpretive work in IPE is directly or indirectly inspired by Marxist and neo-Marxist analyses of capitalism, liberalism, and economic power. Like interpretive work in security, interpretivist IPE attempts to denaturalize dominant forms of power, both historically and in the present. In doing so, its central target is liberalism rather than realism, and it displays tensions between goals of emancipation and deconstruction.

Interpretive work in IPE has, perhaps, a greater tendency to hold onto the idea of one or several material world(s) "out there" than interpretive work in international security, even if these worlds are constitutive of discursive forms of power. This is, I think, because one of the central tasks of interpretivist security studies is to demythologize militarist rationalizations that appear to be highly irrational, whereas interpretivist IPE scholars retain a desire to equalize in some measure the use of resources, reducing both what appear to be obscene levels of wealth accrued by a few, and the sometimes unimaginable struggles for survival on the part of many. Yet feminist scholarship has again led the way in developing concepts and methodological interventions to enhance reflexivity in interpretivist IPE scholarship. The combination of Marxist attention to inequality and feminist attention to gender has also bred tendencies toward victimization of the "subaltern woman" that need to be decentered. Postcolonial theory, along with Foucauldian insights, have been productively employed by interpretivist IPE scholars to engage with the multiple forms of discursive power at issue in different parts of the world, reversing victimhood to look at new forms of intentional agency on the part of marginalized actors and new forms of reflexivity on the part of scholars. Each of these developments entails ethical commitments to expose and disrupt, at a minimum, or to change in favor of a vaguely defined "better" alternative, at a maximum, unequal relations of power. These commitments are an integral part of interpretivist scholarship in international political economy.

Looking forward, the dual commitments to exposing power and deepening reflexivity are resulting in work that focuses on potential changes in the character and dynamics of neoliberalism, even rejecting that term as too global and undiscriminating in character, and incorporating more detailed analyses of the meaning of new domains of property ownership and commodification in ever-expanding virtual worlds. Future interpretivist IPE will likely continue these trajectories, while broadening the geographic and temporal scope of alternative economic histories and their political implications.

Notes

1   "Gold standard and constitutionalism were the instruments which made the voice of the City of London heard in many smaller countries which had adopted these symbols of adherence to the new international order. The Pax Britannica held its sway sometimes by the ominous poise of heavy ship's cannon, but more frequently it prevailed by the timely pull of a thread in the international monetary network." Karl Polanyi, 1944/57, *The Great Transformation: the political and economic origins of our time*, Boston: Beacon Press, 14.

2   Neoliberalism has become an overused term, but generally refers to both the theory and practice of freeing the market from restrictions, including especially those pertaining to government control. It therefore privileges the creation—and distribution—of wealth by market forces, and attempts to reduce government functions to supporting these forces rather than redistributing wealth or using revenue to provide for social welfare programs. See, for example, David Harvey, 2005, *A Brief History of Neoliberalism*, Oxford University Press.

4

INTERPRETING INTERNATIONAL LAW AND ORGANIZATION

What are international law and organization for interpretivists? Do they matter, and if so, how?

What are rules and norms and what is their meaning in international politics?

What is the relationship between dominant narratives of global order, experiences of colonialism, and the ethics of international law and organization?

What is the meaning of cosmopolitanism for international law and organization, and what, if any, are the alternatives to it?

Convention treats international law and international organization as two different subfields of IR. Yet in many ways they are so symbiotically related that it does not make sense to separate them for the purposes of this book. International organizations, from the League of Nations to the United Nations to international agencies such as the International Monetary Fund and the International Bank for Reconstruction and Development (IBRD, or World Bank), came out of the progressive era push to codify and organize social relations at all levels—family, domestic, and international—and they rely on charters and legal codes for their procedural and normative existence. While aspirations for the "rule of law" underpinned the foundations of the field of IR (as noted in Chapter 2), these aspirations depended on the establishment of formal organizations—the Permanent Court of International Justice (PCIJ), the League of Nations, and later the UN and its member agencies.

IPE and international organization are also closely related sub-fields, demonstrated by the creation of organizations to manage global finance and trade, such as the nineteenth-century gold standard, the mid-twentieth-century Bretton Woods institutions, and the 1995 World Trade Organization (WTO) (see Murphy 1994 on the political economy of international organization). In addition, much contemporary critical work on human rights and humanitarianism connects these forms of law to trends in neoliberal political economy. International security and international law and organization are also closely tied, because law was supposed to regulate violence and enhance security, and organizations and issue-area regimes beginning with the 1815 Concert of Europe were the means through which states could discuss tensions and collaborate on rule-bound initiatives to tame them. Moreover, interpretivist studies in law and organization in the 1980s gained influence precisely because they challenged many of the central tenets of neorealist security approaches—norms, rules, and legal conventions underpinned important security relationships. Yet neither of these subfields is as symbiotically connected as law and organization, which is why I examine them together in this chapter.

The question about what problems law and organization might resolve begs the issue of ethics, although IR scholars during the Cold War appeared to take pains to ignore ethical questions (on the dearth of normative theory in IR, see Frost 1996). If law and organization are supposed to regulate and tame war, provide order, and promote justice, how do they do so and to what ends? What types of ethics are involved in attempts to spread "the rule of law" and establish international organizations? More specifically, are ethics that are deontological (driven by principle alone) or consequentialist (based on the expected outcome of action) possible or desirable to establish despite significant cultural, political, economic and social differences among peoples of the world? In other words, can ethics be truly cosmopolitan or global? These questions have given rise to the simplistically framed "cosmopolitan versus communitarian" debate. This chapter, consequently, explores interpretivist IR literatures on cosmopolitanism versus various local/global constructions of normative, legal, and ethical possibility in IR.

Many of the epistemological interventions made by interpretivists began to take hold through the work of scholars specializing in international law and organization. During the heyday of the Cold War, realist scholars laid down the gauntlet by pushing aside international law as "not real law," ineffective, and therefore not worthy of study. Domestic law had sanctions to back it up, but international law had no central governing structure, "Leviathan," or coercive power to support it and compel compliance. International organization, especially for neorealists, was interesting only insofar as it reflected great power relations or hegemonic stability theory, and compliance became a central empirical problem. As A. Claire Cutler (2002: 181) argues, conventional approaches to international politics and law "are dominated by ahistorical and state-centric theories that are incapable of dealing analytically, theoretically and normatively with contemporary transformations in global power and authority." Hedley Bull took on this challenge by arguing that international relations is best understood as an "anarchical society" rather than an ahistorical state system (Bull 1977).

Much of the dismissal of international law and organization had to do with scholars' inability to "prove" its effects using positivist or critical rationalist epistemologies and methodologies. Friedrich Kratochwil and John Ruggie exposed the problematic philosophy of science undergirding such criticisms in a 1986 article, "The State of the Art on an Art of the State," in the journal *International Organization*. This article traced the historiography of the subfield of international organization (with many implications for law) by demonstrating how early twentieth-century studies focused on formal organizations while Cold War (post-Bretton Woods) scholarship focused on the governance of particular, differentiated "issue-areas" such as money, trade, security, human rights, and the environment (Kratochwil and Ruggie 1986; Krasner 1983). More importantly, Kratochwil and Ruggie foregrounded much of the interpretive work in international law and organization that would occur over the subsequent two decades by pointing out a major ontological and epistemological discrepancy in the study of "international regimes" (systems of rules, norms, principles, and procedures governing issue-areas such as trade, proliferation, monetary relations, and the environment, see Chapter 3): that positivist methods of ascertaining whether a "regime violation" had occurred did not allow for the interpretive and persuasive methods employed by interpretivist traditions of jurisprudence, and would therefore lead scholars astray in their attempts to judge the legitimacy and durability of these forms of governance.

Using language theory as well as ontological and epistemological insights, work by international legal scholars including Nicholas Onuf (1989), who pioneered the discussion of "rule" and "rules" in international relations and law, Friedrich Kratochwil (1989), who articulated a jurisprudential understanding of norms and communicative rationality, and Richard Falk (1995), who articulated alternative bases for "world order" (through the "world order models project"), moved international law into the mainstream while complicating the concept of sovereignty (see also Bartelson 1995). These works, along with the rapid development of what became known as the "English School" in IR (see Chapter 2) each promoted constitutive understandings of global governance and international order.

Feminist international law became a thriving subfield within critical legal studies and has made inroads into international relations scholarship, although perhaps not as strongly as feminist scholarship in IPE and international security. Feminist IR theorists, nevertheless, have been at the forefront of developing new ways to understand the gendered nature of international institutions, in the sense of both formal organizations and patterns of practices, and articulating new forms of solidarity, such as an "ethics of care" (Robinson 2011) or a reconfiguring of public/private distinctions in international relations (Lu 2006), to overcome the disempowering features of liberal individualism. Along with the work of critical international law scholars, their research enables a conceptual and empirical broadening of the geographic and socio-cultural scope of legal developments and resistances to them. This chapter also examines, therefore, questions regarding the degree to which law and organization are constitutive of hegemonic and gendered material and ideological power relations produced by military adventurism, colonialism, and technological developments. It begs one of the questions of the final chapter, which is to what degree are other world histories, securities, political economies, and legal and normative institutions ignored by IR theory? And what happens to IR theory if they are included as equals in the "canon" (on authoritative canons in IR, see Brown, Nardin and Rengger 2002)?

Finally, it is likely that consensus can never be reached on what should be the aims of knowledge construction, or the means to peace and security, or the bases of equitable relations among states and societies. The chapter concludes by examining the recommendations of feminist ethical projects and comparing them to recent studies of pragmatism, asking whether either or both suggest productive paths for future scholarship, or whether they provide fodder for yet more debates that will likely prove to be as contentious as those of the past.

Rules, Norms, and Politics in Interpretive International Law and Organization

Thinkers who have articulated and promoted international law—from Thomas Aquinas to Francisco Vitoria to Hugo Grotius to Immanuel Kant and his successors—respond to the problems of order of their times. Vitoria tried to tame the brutality of colonialism in the Americas, but with only limited rights for the colonized. Grotius helped legitimize the expansion of Dutch hegemony through trade by specifying requirements for peace and war, and Kant put forth a deolontological ethics that grappled with social change while promoting a European version of cosmopolitanism. Interpretivists consequently view the results of their endeavors—and those of many others, including Gentili, Vico, Pufendorf, Hobbes, and Locke—as fluid representations of pressing questions articulated in specific historical contexts rather than as fixed mandates. As Onuf points out, there are multiple stories about the development of international law from the ancients to the postmoderns.[1] Yet interpretivist scholars of international law throughout much of the twentieth century found themselves articulating narratives that legitimated the study of law as significant for international relations.

This interpretivist view of law—that it definitely matters, but is not "causal" or "fixed" in any structural or permanent sense—also entails privileging a view of law as *process*. "Law-as-process" arguments are generally inspired by the work of Myers McDougal, Harold Laswell and the New Haven school of law, although Friedrich Kratochwil argues that incorporating the normative dimensions of legal and practical reasoning is required to understand its jurisprudential character. Law and indeed international interactions in general are about providing persuasive *reasons* and justifications for state actions, resulting in an "interpretation of law as a particular branch of practical reasoning" (Kratochwil 1989: 18). Strategic interaction relies on this type of communicative "rationality," but it is not an *a priori* or ahistorical rationality that can be taken out of specific temporal contexts. This is also why the *normative frameworks* of state (and non-state) communications matter in international politics. Norms cannot be seen as "causal" in a narrow sense; instead, they work to "constrain" or "enable" particular types of action.

Nicholas Onuf takes a related yet different approach to arguing in favor of law's significance. Onuf, who brought the term "constructivism" into IR, is concerned with the different types of "rules" that enable social and political interaction, resulting in his famous description of a "world of our making" (Onuf 1989). Drawing on the language theories of Searle and the later Wittgenstein, Onuf asserts that rules parallel "speech-acts" in form and can be classified in three categories according to their function: "instruction-rules" (assertive speech-acts that provide information and tell agents what they should do with it); "directive-rules" (imperative statements that are "emphatically normative"); and "commitment-rules" (commissive speech-acts in which "speakers make promises that hearers accept") (Onuf 1998: 67). The dominance of any of these categories results in different forms of international order, such that hegemonic rule is produced when instruction-rules predominate, more formal types of hierarchy ensue when more emphatic and normative directive-rules prevail, and the most formalized type of rule, "constitutional rule" , ensues when speakers and hearers accept commitment-rules (Onuf 2013: 11–12). Onuf's interest is to systematize our thinking regarding the linguistic construction of social order, not to theorize a cause-effect relationship between variables. These types of rule, then, are constitutive of speech-acts, which means that they are indeed social constructions. Moreover, the existence of all three types of rules means that IR cannot be characterized by the neorealist conception of "anarchy."

Friedrich Kratochwil also relies heavily on insights from theories of language, but does so to demonstrate both the constraining and enabling power of norms (1989). While he enumerates many of the same normative functions that are comprised in Onuf's construct, he emphasizes the power of intersubjectivity and persuasion in inter-state communications, from security negotiations to monetary relations. This elaboration of the operation of normative and legal language demonstrates, once again, the problematic nature of the neorealist argument that law is nonbinding, with no "real" effects, and that anarchy reins among sovereign states as well as other international actors. Taken together, these insights posed a critical challenge to the fact/value distinction and the correspondence theory of truth in demonstrating that meaning infuses language, and that norms on the international level exist, shaping, enabling and constraining international order, regimes, and law.

These arguments were originally made in the 1980s, breaking through the armor of structural realism's conception of international life as one of anarchy in a system of "self-help." As Kratochwil showed, international "anarchy" depends on conventions, communications, and intersubjective normative guidelines and agreements (Kratochwil 1989). Bringing to light the shared, normatively based character of bilateral and multilateral "signaling," even and perhaps especially among adversaries, moves us in many ways beyond Hedley Bull's conception of the international as an "anarchical *society*" (Bull 1977) and even farther from the idea of a brute anarchy based on purely material power considerations.

These insights from legal theory, language theory and philosophy increasingly infused debates in international organization, which during the 1980s became preoccupied with non-formal transnational governance, conceptualized as "regimes" (Krasner 1983). The same logic that scholars employed to demonstrate the necessity of norms, rules, and law showed the need to study the social nature of regimes and the institutions (or sets of practices) that defined them in order to understand and explicate structures of authority and relations of power in IR. Regimes channeled, exposed, and at times limited the use of power, precisely because of the intersubjective nature of regime norms and rules. As Ruggie argued, we know regimes "by their generative grammar, the underlying principles of order and meaning that shape the manner of their formation and transformation" (Ruggie 1998). As "social institutions around which actor expectations converge" in a particular issue-area (Krasner 1983; Ruggie 1998: 63), regimes provided a spatial and temporal site for communication, action, the exercise of political authority, and the reinforcement of or challenge to shared normative goals among state actors.

Such insights posed significant challenges to attempts to fit the interpretive ontology of regimes into a positivist epistemology for "testing" regime existence and strength. In the United Kingdom, they helped consolidate the English School's epistemology which, taking the work of Martin Wight and Hedley Bull as points of departure, emphasized the shared social nature of international relations at the same time as it articulated a skepticism vis-à-vis the possibility of progress (Dunne 1998; Buzan and Little 2000). In the United States, however, instead of a new interpretivist mainstream developing in IR, the IO/ILaw debate moved from the focus on how to study regimes to a focus on how to study norms. Here again, interpretivist insights eventually became narrowed and channeled into positivist categories to create a cottage industry of work that attempted to separate material from "ideational" or normative factors in promoting change in international law and organization. This narrowing became the focus of conventional constructivist research, and it occurred at least in part due to pressure by neorealists and neoliberals to demonstrate the "value-added" (rather than the constitutive nature) of constructivist insights. The question of whether a given political outcome (e.g., the creation of an institution, the absence or management of conflict) was due to norms, or whether it was due to "material" factors filled many journal pages. The bifurcation of the "ideational" and the "material," however, is precisely what interpretivists reject on philosophy of science grounds: problematizing the fact/value distinction and the correspondence theory of truth requires a constitutive understanding of how objects and events are infused with meaning. Moreover, the focus on the value-added of norms also ignored the insights of language theory (employed by Onuf), which demonstrated the particularities of different types of rules, and their functions in constituting social orders. As a result, interpretivists moved for a time to emphasize metaphysical issues, including the importance of intersubjective and relational ontologies for conceptualizing research topics, and post-structural (and hence interpretivist) epistemologies for explicating the fluid and changing nature of global processes and outcomes.

The next generation of interpretivist law and organization scholars brought questions of discursive power, types of world order, ethics, and agency more centrally into focus. Kratochwil's early work tended to make secondary the question of what kinds of ethics constituted international norms and law (Lynch 2010), while Onuf focused on the philosophical and rule-based content of republicanism, including its critics and contradictions (Onuf 1998), and theorists such as Terry Nardin emphasized the significance of positive law in enabling international agreements (Nardin 1983). But these contributions begged questions regarding the meaning and ethics of rule, norms, order, and law. Interpretive work on norms and discourse, as well as interpretive critical and postcolonial work, increasingly brought ethical and moral issues to the forefront in a variety of issue-areas and historical temporalities.

For example, one set of questions for interpretivists in international law and organization concerned historical orders, both over the "longue durée" and within specific eras, including what types of ethics as well as institutions predominated and how they were constitutive of systems of authority and legitimacy. Concepts such as the "moral purpose" of states that shape world order, according to Reus-Smit (1999), require an understanding of international "constitutional orders" that base fundamental institutions, including sovereignty, on ethics that need to be understood in their historical context. Thus ancient Greece, Renaissance Italy, absolutist Europe, and liberal modernity are each based on constitutive relationships between moral purpose and constitutional orders. Constitutive relationships also shape "national" identities, as the work of Alexander Wendt demonstrated in the early 1990s (Wendt 1992; see also Hall 1999). A major issue for interpretivist work in this genre, however, concerned how to acknowledge the social construction and power of "national" identity while at the same time understanding identity as multiple and fluid (Bially-Mattern 2005). Again, epistemological and methodological tensions tended to separate interpretivist analyses from more positivistically oriented ones. Interpretivist work on national identity is characterized by a focus on the mechanisms of discursive power in shaping national identities, as well as how identities make possible some knowledge constructions—and therefore policies—over others, but do not "cause" them in a narrow sense (see also Weldes, Laffey, Gusterson, and Duvall 1999).

Global environmental politics was one of the more interesting "regime" issue-areas in which pressing questions regarding discourse, agency and ethics arose. How to manage "public goods" in the "global commons," through mechanisms such as the Law of the Sea treaties and conventions on the exploration of outer space, were important topics for regime theorists, who explored the content, conditions, and probability of international environmental agreements

(Oran Young 1983). But interpretivist environmental theorists also pushed forward research agendas that examined the constitutive role of discursive power in shaping conceptions of environmental stability and harm. Conventional understandings and expectations about state "interests" were ruptured by new types of actors, in particular transnational groups of scientists ("epistemic communities"), who injected technical knowledge into political debates and helped overturn state resistance to environmental treaties such as the Montreal Protocol to halt ozone depletion (Litfin 1994; see also Lipschutz and Conca 1993). But interpretivists also showed how scientific knowledge is subject to politicization, and that scientists also cannot exit from the hermeneutic circle in constructing their research agendas. This central insight of interpretivist research on epistemic communities also led to additional work that examined the genealogies, contradictions, and tensions in the construction of scientific, economic, and popular discourses that shape global environmental politics, such as the change in discursive strategies on whaling from a constitutive component of national identity and power to an immoral destruction of an endangered species (Epstein 2008). Such projects demonstrate the "new subjectivities" (following Foucault) that are created by shifts in ethics that accompany shifts in power and knowledge (see also Luke 1997), and bring social movements and nongovernmental organizations into critical analysis.

Critical and Postcolonial Scholarship on Law and Organization

These debates in IR also took place during an era in which critical legal studies became influential in many law schools in the United States and abroad. In particular, the work of David Kennedy at Harvard inspired a generation of critical legal theorists, who probed the contradictions and nuances of international law's liberal, hegemonic, and "Western" pretenses to foundationalism. A crucial component of Kennedy's project was to critique international law's cosmopolitan and universalist assumptions, which tend to be articulated and codified in ways that deny or stunt "the political" and reinforce (false) foundationalist claims (Kennedy 2000; Lynch and Loriaux 2000).

At issue, then, is how international law, in attempting to solve the problems of political difference, most often reinforces it through unquestioned assumptions and the belief that legal techniques can depoliticize processes of negotiation, mediation, and arbitration. Yet, as Gramsci, Foucault, and other social theorists have warned, the attempt to depoliticize simply masks instead of eliminates the workings of unequal power relations. What is required instead is "an interrogation of the historical processes through which dominant approaches to international law (and international relations) both create and perpetuate social injustices and repressive interests and then make them appear as neutral and objective ontological conditions" (Cutler 2002: 182).

The major historical and contemporary issue for this interrogation of "repressive interests" focuses on the workings of order and law in the "postcolony" (Mbembe 2001) from colonialism through the present. A number of interpretivist IR scholars have taken up the charge of exposing the inequities and Orientalist assumptions behind "Western" international law and imperial order. Roxanne Lynn Doty showed how the discursive representations of populations in the Philippines by the United States, and in Kenya by the British, enabled colonialism and shaped the postcolonial relationships and ongoing power inequities between these countries (Doty 1996), while Kevin Dunn focused on the successive discursive "imaginings" of the Congo that enabled brutal, racially defined conquest by the Belgians, and later, ongoing repression by Mobutu (who was promoted by Western powers), under the guise of anti-communism (2003; see also Autesserre 2010 on top-down international "solutions" for the Congo). Siba N'Zatioula Grovogui demonstrated that such representations continue to be alive and well in detailing the Western-controlled process which led to the independence of Namibia, which was finally achieved only in 1990. This process did not fulfill the progressive, liberal promise of the UN Charter but instead created "Sovereigns, Quasi-Sovereigns, and Africans" (Grovogui 1996). Grovogui argues that legal settlements invariably use Western powers as "brokers" who have strong interests in denying full sovereignty to colonial and formerly colonial territories.

How are these "discursive landscapes" (Dunn 2003) and representations of colonial subjects (Doty 1996) made possible? According to Grovogui, international law itself embodies particular (Western) notions of sovereignty that subjugate the norms and practices of former colonies to those of their colonizers. Moreover, the dominant norms and practices of the colonizers were embodied in mechanisms of international mediation, beginning with the Mandate System under the League of Nations (which brought areas of the Middle East and former German colonies in Africa under the control of France and Britain, the "mandatory powers") and continuing with the creation of the United Nations Charter. As a result, according to Grovogui, "Both the structures of international law and the strictures of international mediation under the UN Charter were inconsistent with African ideals of decolonization," which included "the reestablishment of African sovereignty and the realization of self-determination." These norms and practices enabled Western mediators to act *for* Namibians. They claimed "the rights and privileges historically associated with sovereignty and self-determination and, as in the times of conquest and colonization, subjugated African claims." Sovereignty for Namibians, in this construct, could only be accomplished in the context of ensuring the interests of former colonial powers.

> In effect, Western mediators of the Namibian dispute grounded the rules of decolonization primarily in historically constituted views of their own interests (including postcolonial hegemonic aspirations) that were only

secondarily designed to implement self-determination and sovereignty within the international order.

(Grovogui 2000: 176)

The power of discourse in shaping postcolonial relationships and stacking the deck against full sovereignty for states that achieved independence during the twentieth century is, therefore, strong. Yet some argue that the question of whether the colonized also wield power needs to enter the analysis more fully. Lily H.M. Ling examines the West's colonial and postcolonial relations with East Asia, arguing that this relationship has been mutually transformative: while Western discursive constructions and desires created idealizations of East Asian cultures and peoples, competing understandings of hegemony and hierarchy ultimately produced forms of "heteronomy" (Ling 2002). Ling's work raises questions about how political, social, and cultural practices characteristic of different regions can both confront and intersect with each other, transforming conventional self/other distinctions despite inequalities of power. The postcolony, therefore, is not a passive recipient of political, economic, and cultural forms of hegemony, but represents multiple sites of resistance and multiple ways of reshaping power, subjectivity, and identity.

Constructing Subjectivity and Revealing Agency in International Law and Organization

Ling's conclusions might be more characteristic of the colonial encounter in Asia than in Africa, but they also indicate the necessity of understanding the complexity of subjectivities in the Global South as well as in transnational analyses of gender, class, race, and religion (on the last two, see Chapter 5). Interpretivists tend to view subjectivities as constituted both by discursive forms of power (including material as well as ideational or ideological elements) and the participation of agents. The latter, however, can be more or less intentional.

Interpretivists continue to grapple with the "agent-structure problem" (Wendt 1987) and the question of how much intentionality is possible in the construction of identities and subjectivities. In conventional international relations agency was most frequently assigned to the state; this was true even of the first generation of interpretivist law and organization studies. Especially since the end of the Cold War, however, attention to multiple non-state actors, including nongovernmental organizations, religious groups, private health care providers and military contractors, and the media, among others, has skyrocketed. In part this is due to the exponential increase in numbers and kinds of non-state actors themselves (especially NGOs and contractors providing what were formally state services). And, as a number of specialists in international law have pointed out, lawyers, too, are agents. Interpretivists, however, tend not to focus on whether lawyers are the primary agents in achieving specific goals (as in Finnemore 2004), but rather on how they argue and interpret texts in their attempt to persuade, and what these practices reveal about broader social order, rules, and norms (Kratochwil 1989, Onuf 2012). The latter emphasis places lawyers within the hermeneutic circle and prioritizes discursive contestation; the former sees lawyers more as variables in a causal relationship.

This change in orientation regarding who the significant actors in global governance are has produced an attempt by interpretivists to differentiate their studies of agency from those of "liberal" scholars. For example, the growth of humanitarian action can be analyzed as proceeding from non-state actors' efforts to relieve suffering, promote human rights, and ensure post-conflict transitions to justice. Many interpretivists, however, also see this trend as emanating from the retreat of the state in providing social welfare, even while state funding and control of humanitarian aid operate through "donor agencies" that promote neoliberal norms of self-help and "sustainability" (Sending and Neumann 2006; Lynch 2011). Feminist research also complicates understandings of agency and subjectivity by addressing the mutual constitution of agency and the deeply engrained practices of patriarchy and by working to erase the lines between the agency of the researcher and the research subject.

Resolving Conflict: Agency, Legal Institutions, and Practices in the Postcolonial Era

Scholars have persuasively argued that "transitional justice" or post-conflict international institutions were created because of the normative pressure and organizational work performed by non-state actors. The International Criminal Court (ICC), for example, represents a unique legal innovation created by the Treaty of Rome in 1997 to punish individual perpetrators of crimes against humanity. It exists largely because of intentional agency on the part of civil society actors (Struett 2008), who, after the end of the Cold War, insisted on building on the precedent established at Nuremburg (but subsequently ignored for fifty years) of putting war criminals on trial. The ICC, however, has also been criticized for focusing solely on postcolonial, and more specifically African, leaders' perpetration of war crimes and ignoring charges of war crimes against Western officials (Falk, Juergensmeyer, and Popovski 2012; see also Branch 2007). If, as Grovogui points out, the International Court of Justice (ICJ) works from norms and rules that favor the sovereign power of some over others, what about newer international legal innovations such as the ICC? These debates show once again that the creation of legal instruments is constitutive of discursive forms of power, and that despite civil society agency, representations of postcolonial societies as more violent and less "civilized" continue to shape their use.

Both war crimes tribunals and the creation of the ICC highlight the contemporary trend towards "punishment" rather than management of conflict in international relations and humanitarian law. But, somewhat paradoxically, punishment is not the only discursive solution put forward to resolve conflict. Some of the most interesting contemporary debates in international law and organization concern questions of whether and how to engage in "healing" rather than (or sometimes in addition to) punishment in post-conflict societies. In the post-Cold War era, the notion of punishment has taken on new life through the ICC, various other tribunals, and a renewed emphasis on the Genocide Convention, while healing has been pursued through numerous Truth and (sometimes also) Reconciliation Commissions in Latin America, Africa, Southeastern Europe, and Asia. As a result, a new cottage industry of research on the theme of "transitional justice" has arisen. Much of this work has primarily policy import, in that it attempts to articulate the best practices, techniques, and policies for the restoration of peace after conflict. But for interpretivists, the discourses of transitional justice and the techniques that it encompasses should be topics of interrogation.

Punishment, as Michel Foucault argued several decades ago, can be juxtaposed with the concept of "discipline" to evaluate the mechanisms of discursive power that have been used to maintain social order in the medieval and modern eras. Several scholars have returned to the legacy of punishment and healing to examine their discursive nature and the political conditions that have made them salient in international law and post-conflict modes of organization today (Lu 2006; Lang 2008; Gould 2010). These scholars also highlight debates about the ideals and mechanisms of liberal world order—whether they can and should be "reformed" or whether they are antithetical to global justice and equity.

Catherine Lu, for example, defends a reformulated liberal order, one that provides a different articulation of cosmopolitan ethics. She argues that liberal cosmopolitan's construction of the "public" versus "private" realms of authority actually provides the resources for international humanitarian law to focus on "the duties of cosmopolitan justice" rather than military intervention. This is because, just as privacy is constrained in the "private," family realm by the need to protect individuals, the same goes for constraining state sovereignty in the "public" realm (Lu 2006). Lu's articulation of states' "responsibility to protect" ultimately argues for an ethics that attempts to refashion liberalism rather than to critique or replace it. Liberalism here is not an ahistorical given, but rather a complex of ethical and historically situated meanings that must be explicated and grappled with to achieve particular emancipatory goals.

Yet a major question that interpretivist scholars of law must wrestle with, particularly those who defend contemporary liberalism, is whether the idea of "personhood" should also apply to the state, and if so, what types of obligations follow. Tony Lang links this debate to the concept of punishment—of states as well as individuals—through sanctions and war. He argues that the "domestic analogy" that enables such punishment is wrong and produces unjust effects. "The current [liberal] international order relies on a set of punitive practices" such as "military intervention, economic sanctions, international criminal courts, and counter-terrorist policy." But these punitive practices, he asserts, actually "create more conflict than cooperation." This is because the liberal order they exist within is itself unjust and biased towards the powerful. This is so even though punitive practices are justified by liberal norms of "human rights, democracy promotion and nonproliferation of weapons of mass destruction" (Lang 2008: 3).

Lang partially departs from the tradition of assigning states individual personhood. This tradition, according to Harry Gould, goes back to the Romans but was strengthened by the alliance of Christendom with natural law in the medieval period. State "corporality," however, is an extremely problematic concept, according to Gould, leading to expectations on the part of human rights advocates that state complicity in human rights violations can be sufficiently punished (Gould 2010), although such expectations have never been and cannot be fulfilled.

Punishment, then, is one possible means of redressing "wrongs" in international relations, but who is to be punished (and, of course, how), remain significant questions that beg investigation of historical and ethical meaning. Another possible means of redressing wrongs is the "reconciliation" of adversaries in post-conflict societies, a tool that gained salience on the international level in the 1980s and 1990s and that generally rejects the possibility of punishment in favor of exposing "truth."[2] Like punishment, reconciliation runs into numerous conceptual, ethical, and practical problems, including who is reconciled to whom, what are the discursive effects of distinctions between "victim" and "perpetrator" of violent crimes, and whether "truth" can ever be fully known and acknowledged by all parties.

The use of "truth and reconciliation" commissions has the laudable goal of providing both justice and healing to traumatized individuals and societies. Much has been written about South Africa's Truth and Reconciliation Commission (as well as others) to assess these goals, usually with unsatisfactory results. One of the problems with the attempt to uncover the "truth," like the belief that legal tools and techniques can resolve and possibly eliminate conflict, is that truths are multiple, especially when viewed through the lenses of different peoples' experiences. Moreover, while attempts at "therapeutic justice" can promote useful dialogue about the reasons for systematic violence in post-conflict societies, the techniques employed by truth and reconciliation commissions too often remain sequestered in norms and rules that limit their ability to address exactly these issues. This is why Bronwyn Leebaw, drawing from theorists ranging from Hannah Arendt to Mahmood Mamdani, argues that the experience of transitional justice mechanisms in post-apartheid South Africa demonstrates the need to bring those who resisted apartheid much more centrally into transitional justice processes. Acknowledging the work of resisters to the injustices of the system both complicates definitions of victim/perpetrator and leads to more complete discussion and debate about how to establish justice in the present and future (Leebaw 2011).

While punishment and reconciliation run into conceptual and substantive problems on the international level, explicating resistance is a potentially productive path for interpretivist research to pursue. Given that treatments of resistance have tended to fade into unwarranted obscurity, or become linked exclusively to projects deemed structurally Marxist and therefore utopian, the argument that resistance needs acknowledgment and theoretical treatment is important for thinking through goals of critique and emancipation. It is also critical for future work that assesses the discursive power of human rights and humanitarian law as well as transitional justice mechanisms. This is because the range of ethical sensibilities and actual strategies employed in resistance break down victim/perpetrator dichotomies that also influence these issue-areas. Analyzing resistance can also assist in broadening the normative possibilities of justice and rights frameworks.

Alternatives to Cosmopolitan Pretensions? Feminism and Pragmatism in Law, Organization, Ethics, and World Order

Charges that international law and organizations treat sovereign claims by postcolonial states unfairly beg the question of whether or not law can represent a type of "genuine" cosmopolitan ethics (comprehensively agreed-upon and applied across the globe, and devoid of inequalities), or whether it is always a reflection of hegemonic power relationships (Ishay 1995). Most interpretivist IR scholars, following Walker, caution that

> anyone seeking to reimagine the possibilities of political life under contemporary conditions would be wise to resist ambitions expressed as a move from a politics of the international to a politics of the world, and to pay far greater attention to what goes on at the boundaries, borders and limits of a politics orchestrated *within* the international. . . .
>
> *(Walker 2010: 2–3)*

In other words, the very conditions of possibility of the international, in their intersecting "inside/outside" political dimensions, preclude any global, world, or cosmopolitan ethics. Rather than try to institutionalize such an ethical system, we should focus instead on the micro and macro processes that produce and reinforce exclusion in world order, and hence in international law and organization.

All interpretivist scholars of international law and organization view sovereignty as a social construct and the state as a historically produced "social fact" (Ruggie 1998). Nevertheless, not all interpretivists have given up on either cosmopolitanism or liberalism, although these scholars argue that their ethical bases must be reformulated in order to address exclusions. In the previous chapter, we saw that Michael Loriaux articulated the basis for a type of "regional cosmopolitanism" that would recognize the unique history of the Rhineland's political economy in deconstructing borders to achieve a form of ethical consensus (Loriaux 2008). Regional ethics have been much discussed in other areas of the world, for example in debates about Asian values. Focusing on historical experience in both Asia and Africa, however, brings to light regional histories and practices that complicate Western attempts at ethical hegemony (Ling 2002; Grovogui 2006).

Feminist work on the "ethics of care" (Tronto 1993; Robinson 2011; Hutchings 2010) provides a different reformulation of cosmopolitanism. In foregrounding a relational understanding of responsibility and duty towards others, these feminist scholars reject the individualism of liberal cosmopolitanism. As Fiona Robinson asserts,

> The privatization and denigration of care were crucial features of the rise of liberalism and continue to be constitutive of contemporary liberal ethics and political ideology. Liberalism's emphasis on autonomy, individual rights, and formal-legal equality depends upon the feminization and privatization of care work.
>
> *(Robinson 2011: 164)*

Moreover, liberal "hegemony" (in a Gramscian sense of cultural as well as economic hegemony) convinces women "to assume responsibility for the care of home and children," which enables it to mask and ignore "the contribution made by those it excluded" (Robinson 2011: 164).

Feminist scholars are, however, aware of the difficulties, both conceptual and political, in actualizing a politics and ethics of care. One conceptual pitfall (that many liberal feminists and humanitarians have fallen into) is to turn care into an ethics of "benevolence, charity, or attention to the 'victims' or the 'vulnerable'," a concern that is also central to critics of contemporary humanitarianism (see The Critical Investigations into Humanitarianism in Africa Blog, www.cihablog.com). To counter this potential tendency, Robinson calls for

> reading care within the frame of the colonial encounter, as well as within the context of contemporary global relations of race and geopolitics . . . for a global commitment to care that complicates our understandings of the protectors and the protected, the strong and the vulnerable, while recognizing that shifting relations of dependence and interdependence are a normal feature of social life and global politics.
>
> *(Robinson 2011: 165)*

This "nonidealized conception of care ethics" that Robinson articulates recalls the work of other interpretivist scholars to bring politics and resistance—i.e. justice and equity—into debates about the ongoing nature of world order and global governance.

Work on the ethics of pragmatism also moves away from liberal ideals. Molly Cochran, for example, argues in favor of "international ethics as pragmatic critique," bringing together the philosophies of John Dewey and Richard Rorty to address both the critique of liberal foundationalism and the necessity of ethical action in the world (Cochran 1999). Cochran contrasts different types of anti-foundationalism, including "post-structuralist" and "neo-pragmatist," arguing that the latter provides a more fruitful basis for ethical critique that can also incorporate moral imagination and the inclusion of feminist concerns about gendered (and therefore biased) ethical constructs of both cosmopolitanism and communitarianism. As Kratochwil asserts, pragmatism should not be thought of as finding a lowest common denominator of agreement when various theories have come up empty. Instead, the "pragmatic turn" rejects the attempt to reduce "issues of *praxis,* and of the knowledge appropriate for it, to 'philosophical' or even metaphysical questions" (Kratochwil 2011: 200–201). Marx, for example, in his "Theses on Feuerbach," argued against divorcing praxis, or "human sensuous activity," from purely theoretical constructions to focus instead on its "practical" meaning for revolutionary activity (Marx 1967). What pragmatism does emphasize, rather than metaphysics, then, is action, pluralism, and analytical eclecticism.[3]

The pragmatic turn in some ways sums up interpretivist research trajectories on issues of world order, global governance, law and organization. This is because it "ties in with and feeds into the linguistic, constructivist and 'historical' turns that preceded it." It also "reminds us that 'truth' and meaning are, however, not problems of simple reference, but problems of relation with other concepts in a semantic field, and of linking the problem under investigation to actions and practices which are the stuff of 'politics'" (Kratochwil 2011). Whether it is sufficiently robust in terms of content to satisfy interpretivist goals of emancipation as well as critique, however, remains a question for future research to determine.

Interpretivism in International Law and Organization

Interpretivists in international law and organization reconceptualized world order, including legal processes, as social constructions, thereby challenging neorealist assumptions about international structure. They conceptualized norms (Kratochwil 1989) and rules (Onuf 1989) as central to the linguistic composition of different forms of order as well as the ongoing practices that reproduce and challenge them. From the beginning, then, interpretivists working in the area of law and organization have based their work on insights stemming from the linguistic turn in the philosophy of science, especially regarding the difficulties of assuming a correspondence theory of truth in analyzing international relations of power and order.

Additional research probed questions regarding the discursive forms of power constituted by international practices of "reconciliation" and "transitional justice" in attempts to resolve ongoing conflicts. Further, postcolonial scholars demonstrated how these practices were symbiotically related to colonial systems of rule and constructions of Otherness. The racialized implications of these systems will be discussed in the next chapter, but this chapter also addressed the problematic pretenses to cosmopolitan ethics that result from transnationalized, liberal norms and forms of governance.

Interpretivists in international law and organization tend to be critical of liberal cosmopolitan ethics, yet some find it difficult to exit from liberal pretenses given their positionality within the hermeneutic circle. Postcolonial and feminist scholars attempt to exit through critique and deconstruction, or emancipation through constructing a more historically sensitive, contextualized, and relational ethics of care. Pragmatists, instead, focus on *Verstehen,* through the constant evaluation of multiple ways of acting in the world. Practicing pluralism and reflexivity, in addition to continued attempts to develop situated ethics that can transcend injustices, are likely to remain sites of interpretivist explorations into international law and organization in the future.

Notes

1   The usual story, however, is that Grotius was the "father" of international law, bringing "naturalism" to the prior dominance of Catholic universalist theology, and that naturalism eventually gave way to "positivist" international law at the end of the eighteenth century. Onuf, 2002: 26–45, "'Tainted by Contingency': Retelling the Story of International Law," in Richard Falk, Lester Edwin J. Ruiz, and R.B.J. Walker (eds), *Reframing the International: Law, Culture, Politics,* New York: Routledge.

2   Some investigations only purport to uncover "truth," while others—which I focus on here—view the discovery of "truth" as a necessary pre-requisite to "reconciliation."

3   For an analysis and examples of analytic eclecticism that do not foreground interpretive insights, see Rudra Sil and Peter J. Katzenstein (eds), 2010, *Analytic Eclecticism in the Study of World Politics,* New York: Palgrave Macmillan. Indeed, some commentators are using the concept as yet another kind of "third way" (like conventional constructivism before it) between rationalisms and interpretivisms of various kinds.

5

RACE, RELIGION, HISTORIES, AND FUTURES IN INTERNATIONAL RELATIONS

What are interpretivist understandings of race and religion in IR, and how do they challenge conventional meanings across IR subfields?

What are fruitful ways to conceptualize and analyze "otherness" in international relations, in the context of both race and religion?

What types of alternative histories of IR exist, and how might they change the course of future interpretivist research in IR?

This chapter brings together some of the intersecting work that does not fit neatly into the above subfields to allow more explicit attention to race, religion, secularisms, alternative histories of IR, and continuing issues in globalization. Race has continually surfaced in the chapters of this volume because interpretivist work on the causes of imperialist wars, inequities in the global distribution of wealth, and biases in international legal instruments cannot ignore it. Religion—and its secular "other"—were ignored until the late 1990s by critical as well as conventional international relations, and then emerged as a factor almost exclusively in security debates regarding the causes of post-Cold War conflict. Ironically, however, religion—and secularism—are now major topics in IR, although they still sit uneasily in conventional subfields other than security, while issues of race continue to be pushed to the sidelines by liberal cosmopolitan pretensions.

According to interpretivist insights, both race and religion can be analyzed within identity frameworks for research, but there are costs to remaining within an exclusively identity paradigm. As feminist theorists assert, "adding and stirring" a given identity, be it gender, class, race, or religion, risks marginalizing it, or worse yet, lapsing into studies that try to pit one identity against another. Given interpretivists' more holistic conceptual and substantive orientations, such parsing is problematic. Consequently, this chapter examines work that draws out the discursive, contextual, and historical power relationships that produce representations of race and religion.

A deeper examination of race and religion in IR inevitably begs the question of non-Eurocentric conceptualizations of world politics. This chapter therefore notes current research on alternative world histories and asks how these might reshape our conceptions of IR as well as open new avenues for future work.

Is Racism Embedded in the History of the International Relations Discipline?

A 2011 report by the American Political Science Association asserts that the field of political science insufficiently addresses critical questions regarding race (APSA 2011). In international politics, race has arguably been dispositive in motivating conquest and colonization throughout the modern era. Yet, despite the fact that studies of colonialism, postcolonialism, and globalization frequently challenge problematic representations by Westerners of races and ethnicities characteristic of peoples in the Global South, race is only recently moving to the forefront of even critical international relations scholarship. It is all the more imperative for interpretive international relations to address the assumptions that enable and authorize racial categories and conceptions of otherness.

Ido Oren's research on the foundations of the discipline is instructive (Oren 2003; see also Chapter 2). This case and others beg the question of race and how it shapes the nexus between power and knowledge. Robert Vitalis's work, in particular, demonstrates that the fields of political science, IR, sociology and anthropology, were all marked by beliefs in the superiority of white, Western "races." This belief in racial superiority represents, Vitalis argues, the very condition of possibility for the creation and development of these fields of knowledge (Vitalis 2010). Racial constructions, moreover, were intimately related to the belief in the progressive accumulation of knowledge that characterizes positivism, feeding the idea that social characteristics could be specified and analyzed according to biological, and hence "scientific," criteria. This is not to assert that interpretive work inherently avoids the serious problem of imputing value and status to racialized (and racist) categories: indeed, some classical realists articulated extremely problematic assumptions about race (Vitalis 2010; Oren 2003), and the problematic discourses of contemporary humanitarianism can envelop scholars of all epistemological and methodological orientations. But interpretivist insights regarding the positionality of the researcher in the context of her research, and interpretivist exhortations regarding the importance of adopting and maintaining a reflexive stance throughout the research process, can assist in providing at least a partial check on racialized constructions of otherness.

The Critique of Alterity in International Relations

Disciplinary assumptions enabled policies that promoted "civilizing missions" and control over racialized Others well into the twentieth century; these forms of control are arguably perpetuated in discourses regarding the International Criminal Court, human rights, and development and humanitarian aid today. Interpretivist scholars of race in IR employ critical insights from the work of Franz Fanon and Edward Said, as well as social theorists including Emanuel Levinas, Antonio Gramsci, Stuart Hall, and Jacques Derrida (Campbell 1998; Doty 1996) to understand these assumptions and policies. Fanon, whose revolutionary consciousness came out of his work in Algeria during its civil war against France, pinpointed in no uncertain terms the racist beliefs that justified colonial violence in works such as *The Wretched of the Earth* (1961/2005) and *Black Skin, White Masks* (1967). Said, a Palestinian exile who constantly navigated between "Western" and "Eastern" histories and subjectivities, forcefully articulated the symbiotic connections between academic knowledge and racialized constructions of otherness in his seminal work, *Orientalism* (Said 1979).

Fanon's searing portrayal of racism rips apart the liberal edifice that links its own violence with reason and the violence of others with irrationality and backwardness. As Himadeep Muppidi explains, Fanon exposed modern liberals' false conviction that "*their* violence is of a different sort—one backed by Reason." This conviction rationalizes "colonial interventions in seemingly illiberal countries in order to promote democracy, foster human rights, promote sustainable development, rescue women or many other such causes." The "intimacy and complicity" between empire and modern liberalism "makes the indignity of colonialism invisible to the modern world" (Muppidi 2009: 154).

In exposing this complicity, Fanon demonstrated that colonial rule was not "Reason but . . . the structuring of a specific world order—a violent structuring that must be rejected by 'all means necessary'," including revolution (Fanon 2004: 23, cited in Muppidi 2009:150–160). This problem of liberal violence has also been pursued by Mahmood Mamdani and Talal Asad, among others. Mamdani, for example, argues that modern liberalism distinguishes between violence "that appears senseless, that cannot be justified by [liberal notions of] progress," even if it is pervasive and all-encompassing, and violence that is performed by Others who cannot be labeled liberals (Mamdani 2004: 4, quoted in Muppidi 2009: 154), while Asad juxtaposes the violence that justifies aerial bombing, which destroys entire villages in Vietnam or Iraq, with that of suicide bombers who aim to instill terror in Western as well as non-Western populations (Asad 2007). In each of these situations, the colonial self must always, as Fanon insisted to Jean-Paul Sartre, engage in a sort of defensive reflexivity, "constantly aware of his position, his image," and of threats "from all sides" (de Beauvoir, quoted in Bhabha 2005: vii). Fanon positions the colonized people as inextricably caught up in liberal violence, with the resulting choice of being complicit in its maintenance or actively resisting its reproduction (Fanon 1961/2005).

Said, in partial contrast, highlights the complicity of knowledge construction on the part of academics, diplomats, travel writers and novelists from the "West" in creating and perpetuating mythological identities for entire populations in the non-West, and particularly the Middle East. The power of the resulting narratives in constituting Otherness enabled colonial conquest and domination and continues to animate beliefs in white, Western superiority. These narratives became part and parcel of the imperial project, re-inscribing "Orientals" (i.e., Middle Eastern populations) as "really" possessing particular and often contradictory characteristics (e.g. cunning and dishonesty, yet naïveté and ignorance, femininity yet ultra-sexualized masculine imagery). The discursive power of these representations and imposed identities justified the West's "civilizing power" over entire populations, thereby enabling conquest and continuing postcolonial interventions.

Said's work, along with Fanon's, inspired the field of postcolonial studies (see also the discussion of Spivak in Chapters 1 and 3). Yet many interpretivists (as well as liberals) have also criticized Said's conceptualization of orientalism for not taking into account the agency of the colonized, instead treating them as passive subjects, unlike Fanon in his explicit call to active resistance. In creating passive subjects, as feminist theorists have continually pointed out, scholars risk reducing agency to victimhood, ignoring the numerous modes of resistance that challenge discursive forms of power.

One important implication of Said's work and activism concerns what kind of stance is enabled by the "postcolonial intellectual" who occupies a liminal space between East/West; North/South; elite/marginalized, Christian/secular, etc. Does such a positioning provide a kind of exit from geographically defined institutions and ideologies? Duvall and Varadarajan (2007), for example, accord Said a "hermeneutic of worldliness" that, like the positionality of Spivak, Mamdani, and Fanon, provides uniquely important perspectives on questions of race, Otherness, and marginalization. It is probably no accident that each of these scholars was or is engaged as a morally situated "activist" as well as scholar, constantly negotiating and attempting to transcend the boundaries of place and hierarchy to break out of, rather than reproduce, the power relations of the former colonialists who shaped, at least partially, their existence.

This is why some interpretivists in IR have returned to what they call Said's "contrapuntal" (literally, "point against point") methodology, which refers to his relentless navigation, or "traveling theory," across intellectual tensions and paradoxes (Duvall and Varadarajan 2007). These paradoxes include the theoretical examination of "the nature and conduct of critique and its practical relationship to power" (drawing on Foucault) vis-à-vis the scholar's own "performance of 'being critical'—how to think and act critically" (Duvall and Varadarajan 2007: 84). Said's legacy is both to expose and critique the construction of Otherness, especially race, in the encounters of "the West" with "the East," and in so doing to delegitimize both xenophobic and cosmopolitan claims that privilege white,

Western metanarratives about civilization and progress, and to support secular movements for Palestinian liberation. How to theorize a kind of "humanism" without being universalist, and how to reject the construction of national identities while supporting a cause framed in nationalist terms, was not only the paradox of Said's intellectual and activist life, but also a central conundrum for engaged interpretivist scholars. As a result, Said's contemporary interlocutors in IR continue to debate whether interpretive scholarship should rest content with his contrapuntal methodology, or "this condition of being caught in-between by 'at least' two cultures" (even if being in this liminal space also provides knowledge of different kinds of experience), or instead whether scholarship should examine and even "celebrate the richness, resilience, and resonance of overlapping, interactive, mutually creating worlds" (Ling 2002: 139–141). In the first case, difference coexists uneasily although potentially productively, while in the second, difference melds into new forms of identity and experience. The question of alterity, posed through constructions of race and religion (as we shall see below), thus raises questions regarding the experience and possibility of hybridity and syncretism.

Said's contrapuntal methodology is useful for understanding the dilemma of Otherness and the uncertain implications of political engagement. Taken together, Fanon and Said pose questions for IR theorists regarding the injustices, overt cruelties, and wide-ranging forms of oppression and violence that agents, acting in discursively constructed contexts in international politics, have inflicted on racially constituted Others. These forms of oppression and violence are perpetuated by allegedly "neutral" institutions and practices, which pose significant challenges for the task of reconceptualizing subfields of security, political economy, and law and organization (Persaud and Walker; special issue of *Alternatives* 2001). In other words, they require critique and deconstruction to become denaturalized and to enable alternatives to be seen as possible.

Religions, Secularisms, and the Mythologies of Progress

Not only do interpretivist scholars return to race and alterity to explicate the constitution of international relations historically and today, they also address the mythological constructions of the "secular age" (Taylor 2007). Once again the end of the Cold War provides an important marker. The outbreak of conflicts deemed "religious" and "ethnic" prompted questions about the "resurgence" of religion internationally. In IR, these questions manifested themselves in assertions that religion—or at least some religions—caused violence (Huntington 1996).

Interpretivist scholars were quick to point out that these assertions rested on *a priori* assumptions and problematic categorizations (Hatzopoulos and Petito 2000 and 2003; Lynch 2000; Thomas 2000 and 2005; Kubálková 2000). They argued that the clash of civilizations thesis was not well documented, targeted Islam, and essentialized and simplified religious identities, making them primordial, with racist connotations. Scholars in the Copenhagen School argued that religious identities had become "securitized" (Laustsen and Wæver 2000; Sheikh 2011), and anti-Islamic discourse had replaced the anti-Soviet discourse of the Cold War (Esposito 1999). Moreover, the post-Cold War emphasis on the religion/ violence nexus was based on Enlightenment assumptions regarding the superiority and pacific nature of secularism, assumptions that were especially problematic given the conflagrations of the First and Second World Wars (Thomas 2000, 2005; Lynch 2000, 2009). Finally, the "secularization thesis" that linked secularism to progress and peace did not acknowledge the "political theology" of the field of IR (Kubálková 2000), and it completely ignored the longstanding assumptions and taken-for-granted implications of the "politics of secularism" in the field (Shakman Hurd 2008). As a result, the "religious/secular binary" needs to be deconstructed to expose the ongoing relationship between disciplinary power and knowledge construction, on the one hand, and the disciplining of religion through public policies and dominant narratives, on the other (Shakman Hurd 2008).

These interventions from critical constructivist, English School, securitization, and political theory perspectives inform much contemporary interpretive work on religion and secularism. Albeit with differing emphases, they view religion and secularism as constitutive of political, economic, social, and cultural processes and practices. They have taken on issues such as the discursive arenas in the pre- and post- 9/11/2001 periods that brought Islam to the forefront of conventional debates, using fluid concepts such as "jihad" to justify invasion, occupation, and new generations of weapons such as drones. Interpretivists working on religion have, consciously or not, entered a kind of long-term engagement against essentializing tropes and tendencies that attempt to legitimize, yet again, rigid constructions of identity and alterity. This engagement requires constant rebuttals of tendentious claims, while at the same time acknowledging that some actors interpret their own religious (or secular) mandates as justifying if not requiring violence (see Sheikh 2011 for an excellent discussion of such interpretations on the part of Pakistani Taliban groups). Throughout this engagement, interpretivists take pains to contextualize their religious and secular subjects temporally and geographically as well as socially, economically, and politically, working against tendencies to analyze in ahistorical and apolitical terms.

Many scholars who charge that the religion/violence nexus has been reified and oversimplified trace the problem to Enlightenment assumptions (Lynch 2000; Thomas 2005; Shakman Hurd 2008). The dominant narrative is that religion caused the bloodshed of the Thirty Years' War, which European nation-states finally resolved through widespread adoption of secular forms of government. These forms of government reflected the power of developing Enlightenment principles of individual reason, rights, and governmental responsiveness to citizens. Religion, in this narrative, produced attachment to an incendiary combination of the magical, emotive, irrational, and dogmatic, while the exercise of individual reason produced rationality and logic. Each religion was inevitably exclusivist, justifying repression and violence against pagans, nonbelievers, and assorted others (all who did not adhere to its tenets), while its absence, increasingly defined as secularism, produced tolerance and the capacity for pluralism. José Casanova has detailed the problematic nature of this metanarrative while showing how it continues to inform assumptions about religion across Western Europe (Casanova 2007).

The simplified Enlightenment narrative also assumes that secularism, defined as the absence of religion in the public sphere, was a necessary condition for the growth of democracy. Yet, the relationship between religion/peace or violence, and religion/democracy still poses conceptual, methodological, and empirical challenges. The task for interpretivists in understanding any connections between religion and violence (or religion and anything) is neither to essentialize religions (or secularisms) nor to treat them as epiphenomenal.

Essentializing religion means treating it as a rigid, unbending, and unevolving primordial identity, or as a fixed ensemble of doctrinal rules that are imposed on adherents externally by a religious authority that is itself understood ahistorically. The hermeneutic quality of all religious guidelines is completely lost in such an approach. Where Islam is concerned, Sheikh, following Hunter, calls this the "neo-Orientalist" interpretation because it imposes not only an identity but specific forms of action that flow from it on Muslims. This "cultural determinist" approach believes that "Muslims think and behave in certain ways because they are Muslims": as Sheikh points out, scholars adhering to this approach urge "strategies of resistance, suppression and containment" of Muslims and Islam (Hunter 1998: 71; Sheik 2011: 16–17).

Interpretivist scholars of religion have articulated several ways out of this conundrum, in addition to deconstructing the religious/secular binary. Two of these, "neo-Weberianism" and the use of securitization theory for understanding religion, draw significantly from sociological and anthropological insights. Talal Asad, for example, has used anthropological insights to change the way not only scholars in his field but also many others view religion, especially including its development as a historical category (Asad 1993). His work deconstructing suicide bombing in comparison to statist forms of terrorism, moreover, expands on Mark Juergensmeyer's concept of "secular nationalism" to account for the silences in academic discourse vis-à-vis the extreme forms of violence enabled if not promoted by the secular Western state (Asad 2007; Juergensmeyer 2008). Securitization theory (discussed in Chapter Two) focuses on how perceptions of threat become "referent objects" that need to be securitized, resulting in defensive and offensive moves to protect against threats or act against those perceived to be threatening. Here again, there is no *a priori* assumption that "religion" as such produces threats or violence. Instead, the theory analyzes what happens when actors extend the perception of threat to new areas, and whether these new areas (in this case, religion) can be "de-securitized."

Neo-Weberianism also understands "religion" to be a historically constructed category that has imposed politicized meanings on some religions more than others, but it moves beyond any assumed connection between religion and violence to emphasize the need to investigate the relationship between faith and ethical action in a wide range of temporal and spatial contexts (Lynch 2009). While it acknowledges the importance of the social–psychological task of understanding the individual rationales that interpret religious guidelines as legitimizing or requiring violence or non-violence, it also explicates religious ethics as constitutive of social, economic, and political practices that require continual interpretation in particular situations. Because no religious doctrine can guide believers to appropriate action in all contexts, what should be done must be *interpreted*. As a result, a neo-Weberian approach conceptualizes the process of figuring out what to do and how to act as one of "popular casuistry," in which religiously identified individuals and groups derive ethical action from their interpretations of their religious requirements as understood through their political, economic, and socio-historical contexts (Lynch 2009). Neo-Weberianism thus opens the way to understanding how religious norms and practices can be multiple and hybrid (rather than rigid and essentialized), how they can change over time, and how they constitute agents and institutions across subfields in IR, including not only security but law, organization, and political economy.

Alternative Histories and Alternative Futures in International Relations

As of this writing, interpretivist IR scholars are realizing new initiatives to articulate alternative histories of IR from the perspective of actors in Latin America, Africa, East Asia, and the Middle East. What does international history and contemporary theory look like from non-North American and European parts of the globe? What difference does it make to IR to address these histories and perspectives and the conceptual insights that arise from them? This trend to re-envision IR brings together the range of goals in interpretive IR: *Verstehen*, critique, deconstruction, and emancipation.

Conventional IR stories of modernization and secularization, commencing with the Treaties of Westphalia in 1648 and working through the Enlightenment and the Industrial Revolution, present an extremely limited and mythologized view of the "international," which scholars including Siba Grovogui, Arlene Tickner, and Ole Wæver, among others, have been working to rectify. A book series on "Worlding Beyond the West," as well as symposia and special journal issues (see the December 2008 issue of *International Studies Review*), provide material to challenge IR's Eurocentric mythology of origins (see also Shaw and Ashworth 2010). In addition to broadening understanding, these projects work to denaturalize the relationship between "democracy," "human rights," and European and

North American histories (see Grovogui 2006). And they open up the space for new—and potentially more emancipatory—forms of politics, ethics, and participation. Yet, as Tickner has pointed out,[1] the hegemonic pretentions of the discipline of (American and European) IR have also shaped knowledge emanating from other parts of the world. Foucault, Fanon, Spivak, and Gramsci remain critical interlocutors, then, in the attempt to expand our horizons and shed intellectual hegemonies.

Alternative worlds bring alternative narratives which increase the responsibilities of researchers to expand their intellectual horizons. Just as Akira Kurosawa's 1950 movie *Rashomon* is justly famous for bringing the viewer into four different stories of a rape and murder, IR theorists need to sort through persuasive evidence (textual, visual, and experiential) and the multiplicity of contradictions they contain. What "really" happened, either in Kurosawa's film or in a given event in IR? More to the point, what are the reasons for different accounts and what are their implications for the exercise of power and ethics? Self-interest, prestige, gender, class, race, social norms, and prior experience all play into Kurasawa's narrators' attempt to demonstrate "truth" and the audience's attempt to establish meaning. *Rashomon*'s cinematic commentators also situate the film in the context of Japanese devastation and guilt immediately following the Second World War, and the quest for redemption and faith in humanity despite the country's wartime role. According to these commentaries, *Rashomon* is as much about probing the depths of the period, including the interrogation of moral failing, human agency and power, and the desire for faith and hope in the face of destruction and deception, as it is about individual guilt, shame, or innocence.

Interpretivists in IR also confront a multiplicity of narratives, seeking to uncover the possibilities and constraints of power and human agency and acknowledging their own complicity in the stories and meanings they strive to clarify. But how far have interpretivists come and where are they going in these endeavors? One connecting thread throughout this book is the move away from determinisms and towards a range of interpretive possibilities. Acknowledging that there exists not merely a range, but more than one "good" interpretation of events requires a certain scholarly humility. It also foregrounds the relations of power that enable different interpretations to take hold.

Taking seriously issues of race, religion, and alternative histories of IR would likely marginalize Eurocentric and North American perspectives and radically change IR's current emphasis on the transitions from Christian universalism to Enlightenment to "post-secularism," and from multipolarity to bipolarity and back again, to a multiplicity of other narratives, creating new mythologies and moral certainties to deconstruct. It might not challenge as radically, however, critical theory's emphasis on analyzing the transitions from feudalism to capitalism to neoliberalism, but it could re-orient the temporal markers from the Industrial Revolution in Europe to a wide range of political economy transitions in Africa, East and South Asia, Latin America, and the Middle East. More importantly, taking race, religion, and alternative histories seriously should open up a vast array of new questions regarding agency and power across the globe.

Interpretivism and Reflexivity in Studies of Race, Religion, and Alternative Histories and Futures

Expanding IR's geographic and experiential perspectives also requires a return to the concept of reflexivity, which necessitates a commitment to challenge constantly our own and others' assumptions as well as our role as "knowledge creators," citizens of the world and of particular localities, and activists of different kinds. An increasing number of interpretivists in IR are turning to the work of Pierre Bourdieu to articulate the bases and modalities of reflexivity in the social sciences (Leander 2008; Bigo 2011). Unlike many feminist theorists, however, Bourdieu, does not view reflexivity as a means to further goals of emancipation (Bigo 2011). Instead, according to Jackson, Bourdieu's reflexivity calls on "the researcher to be aware of the distorting effects of her or his subjectivity," arising from personal identity characteristics such as gender, class, nationality, ethnicity, "the researcher's location in the intellectual field in which they are operating," and "the temptation to 'stand back' and observe the world as if the researcher is somehow not involved in the social processes under observation" (Jackson 2009: 111–112). The hermeneutic circle looms large in this construct. Reflexivity, in other words, entails acknowledgement of complicity (in power relations and the creation of subjectivities) and the duty to figure out what to do about it.

This acknowledgement of complicity, worked out through concepts of the hermeneutic circle, relational concepts that admit multiple truths, and theories of language, discourse, and power, continue to shape the terrain of interpretivist IR work within and across subfields. This terrain permits a confrontation with race and religion, which is necessary for constructing alternatives to the Eurocentric views of IR that continue to prevail in the discipline. Interpretivists still face the task of deconstructing multiple layers of history and meaning regarding each of these intersecting topics, with strong resistances from discursively constructed assumptions that the world is a mostly tolerant place, that racist things happened historically but no longer in the present, that secularism is a good norm for diffusion throughout the world, and that the European vision and instantiation of law, democracy, and human rights provides the only positive role model for world order. Interpretivists interested in analyzing these issues, as well as their own complicity in them, continue to have plenty to do.

Note

1   According to my notes of comments made at an ISA roundtable, ISA Annual Meeting, 2012.

CONCLUDING THOUGHTS

Politics and Engagement in International Relations

As stated in Chapter 1, this book is itself an interpretation of interpretivist work in IR. It is not possible to write an objective treatise on what interpretation "is," who does it, or exactly which epistemological, methodological, and substantive issues it should address. Nevertheless, books like this one are written out of the conviction that it *is* possible to make an intervention that maps a field that others can agree is important, even if they might disagree on some of its contents or parameters. Even more to the point, as I wrote this book I increasingly understood the political value of highlighting interpretive work in IR. As a field, IR represents a series of intersecting sites in which adherents seem to relish labeling, siloing,[1] and frequently silencing work that disrupts powerful metanarratives, or stories about how the world works and why. IR's followers too often mimic elites whose modus operandi is to jockey for relative power in a self-constructed zero-sum world. Interpretivists challenge the metanarratives, the siloing and silencing, and they tend to be particularly good at exposing the nexus of power and knowledge that reproduces militarisms, inequalities, and identities of Otherness "out there" in the world.

In this field, openings are important. This book, therefore, also has a political purpose. To be political is to be engaged, and writing this book is an act of engagement. It provides a kind of genealogy or historiography—even if it can be contested—of interpretivist research that has made a mark in the field. In doing so, it allows scholars and students who have an interest, feel a kinship, or experience an aesthetic inclination toward interpretivism to situate themselves vis-à-vis an established if still amoeba-like body of work. This body of work provides the infrastructure for a robust legitimization of future innovations in interpretivist research. This is why (and how) such a project is important.

Given that bias can be understood as another word for the absence of distinction between fact and value, or for acknowledging one's positionality within the hermeneutic circle, I acknowledge that my bias in determining the contents of the book is towards critical readings of power and constructions of identity. I navigate between goals of critique, deconstruction, and emancipation towards an as yet unrealized alternative ethics in my own work. But bias is also a relative term, and there is a considerable difference between work that recognizes its hermeneutic positioning and engages in reflexivity, constantly re-examining its conceptual scaffolding and ethical presuppositions vis-à-vis its evidentiary building materials, and work that does not. I hope it is obvious that this book militates in favor of the former and not the latter.

Increasingly, interpretivist research in IR, as recounted in these pages, has moved to incorporate, embrace, and sometimes insist upon the pursuit of reflexivity as part of the scholarly process. This insistence stems from the interpretivist tenets outlined in Chapter 1. Indeed, the explicit recognition of some or all of these tenets has marked the genealogy of interpretivist work in IR from the early twentieth century to the present. In the past, interpretive scholarship reflected on the "big questions" of meaning: of human nature, the content of prudential action, the inevitable partiality of the moral gaze in international politics. Since that time (which might well be taking on a mythological character), the field has moved towards ever-greater specificity in spelling out the logical and social–theoretical foundations of interpretivist concepts and precepts. Over the past two decades, interpretivists in IR have begun to specify even further the step-by-step details of their methods, including various forms of discourse analysis (e.g. from articulation to interpellation; from subjectivity to identity), genealogy, participant-observation and ethnography, as well as describe in ever-greater detail the sources and means of intertextual analysis.

These trends, in my view, are constructive overall, but they must also be understood in the context of ever-greater pressures for specification that come with their own set of problems. Interpretivists have the conceptual background, if anyone does, to understand that these pressures are historically specific and do not necessarily lead, in the end, to "better" knowledge production and accumulation. This is why I have emphasized the intersection between substantive questions that animate interpretivist research, conceptual articulations that help to situate and understand them, and ethical reflections in the form of reflexivity about interpretive processes and goals, rather than attempting to articulate interpretivist "best practices." While interpretivists can never completely avoid the need to specify and improve our practices (nor should they, in my view). This volume, therefore, leaves the way open to continued reflection and articulation, even while it celebrates the impressive volume of interpretivist work that has been researched and written.

Note

1   I am indebted to Nick Onuf who, after questioning this word, then googled it and provided the following definition of "information silo" from Wikipedia (May 9, 2013) that is particularly apt for IR. "An 'information silo' is a management system incapable of reciprocal operation with other, related information systems. . . . 'Information silo' is a pejorative expression that is useful for describing the absence of operational reciprocity. . . . Derived variants are 'silo thinking', 'silo vision', and 'silo mentality'."

BIBLIOGRAPHY

Ackerly, Brooke A., Maria Stern, and Jacqui True (eds). 2006. *Feminist Methodologies for International Relations.* Cambridge: Cambridge University Press.

Ackerly, Brooke, and Jacqui True. 2010. *Doing Feminist Research in Political & Social Science.* New York: Palgrave Macmillan.

Adler, Emmanuel, and Vincent Pouliot (eds). 2011. *International Practices.* Cambridge: Cambridge University Press.

Alcoff, Linda. 1988. "Cultural Feminism v. Post-Structuralism: The Identity Crisis in Feminist Theory," *Signs* 13, 3: 405–436.

Alker, Hayward. 1996. *Rediscoveries and Reformulations: Humanistic Methodologies for International Relations.* Cambridge: Cambridge University Press.

APSA. 2011. *Political Science in the 21st Century.* Report of the Task Force on Political Science in the 21st Century. Washington, DC: American Political Science Association.

Asad, Talal. 1993. *Genealogies of Religion: Discipline and Reasons of Power in Christianity and Islam.* Baltimore: Johns Hopkins University Press.

Asad, Talal. 2007. *On Suicide Bombing.* New York: Columbia University Press.

Ashley, Richard K. 1988. "Untying the Sovereign State: A Double Reading of the Anarchy Problematique," *Millennium: Journal of International Studies* 17, 2: 227–262.

Ashley, Richard K., and R.B.J. Walker. 1990. "Speaking the Language of Exile: Dissident Thought in International Studies," *International Studies Quarterly* 34, 3: 259–268.

Ashworth, Lucian M. 2008. *International Relations and the Labour Party: Intellectuals and Policy-Making from 1918–1945.* New York: Tauris Academic Studies.

Autesserre, Séverine. 2010. *The Trouble with the Congo: Local Violence and the Failure of International Peacebuilding.* Cambridge: Cambridge University Press.

Barkawi, Tarak, and Mark Laffey. 1999. "The Imperial Peace: Democracy, Force and Globalization," *European Journal of International Relations* 5, 4: 403–434.

Bartelson, Jens. 1995. *A Genealogy of Sovereignty.* Cambridge: Cambridge University Press.

Bhabha, Homi. 2005. "Foreword," to Franz Fanon, *The Wretched of the Earth.* New York: Grove Press: vii–xlii.

Bially-Mattern, Janice. 2005. *Ordering International Politics: Identity, Crisis, and Representational Force.* New York: Routledge.

Bially-Mattern, Janice. 2011. "A Practice Theory of Emotion for International Relations," in Emmanuel Adler and Vincent Pouliot (eds), *International Practices.* Cambridge: Cambridge University Press: 63–86.

Bigo, Didier. 2011. "Pierre Bourdieu and International Relations: Power of Practices, Practices of Power," *International Political Sociology* 5, 3: 225–258.

Blaney, David L. and Naeem Inayatullah. 2010. *Savage Economics: Wealth, Poverty, and the Temporal Walls of Capitalism.* New York: Routledge.

Booth, Ken. 1997. "Security and Self: Reflections of a Fallen Realist," in Michael C. Williams and Keith Krause (eds), *Critical Security Studies.* New York: Routledge: 83–120.

Branch, Adam. 2007. "Uganda's Civil War and the Politics of ICC Intervention," *Ethics & International Affairs* 21, 2: 179–198.

Brown, Chris, Terry Nardin and Nicholas Rengger. 2002. *International Relations in Political Thought: Texts from the Ancient Greeks to the First World War.* Cambridge: Cambridge University Press.

Bull, Hedley. 1969. "*The Twenty Years' Crisis* Thirty Years On," *International Journal* 24, 4: 625–638.

Bull, Hedley. 1977. *The Anarchical Society: A Study of Order in World Politics.* London: Macmillan.

Burchell, Graham, Colin Gordon, and Peter Miller (eds). 1991. *The Foucault Effect: Studies in Governmentality.* Chicago: University of Chicago Press.

Butterfield, Herbert. 1965. *The Whig Interpretation of History.* New York: W.W. Norton & Company.

Buzan, Barry, and Richard Little. 2000. *International Systems in World History.* New York: Oxford University Press.

Buzan, Barry, Ole Wæver, and Jaap de Wilde. 1998. *Security: A New Framework for Analysis.* Boulder, CO: Lynne Rienner.

Campbell, David. 1992/1998. *Writing Security: United States Foreign Policy and the Politics of Identity.* Minneapolis: University of Minnesota Press.

Campbell, David. 1998. *National Deconstruction: Violence, Identity and Justice in Bosnia.* Minneapolis: University of Minnesota Press.

Carr, E.H. 1939/1946 [1969]. *The Twenty Years' Crisis: 1919–1939. An Introduction to the Study of International Relations.* New York: Palgrave Macmillan.

Carr, E.H. 1967. *What Is History?* New York: Vintage Press.

Casanova, José. "The Problem of Religion and the Anxieties of European Secular Democracy," paper presented at the 25th Jubilee Conference on Religion and European Democracy. Jerusalem, September 2007.

Chin, Christine 2013. *Cosmopolitan Sex Workers: Women and Migration in a Global City.* Oxford: Oxford University Press.

Claude, Inis. 1962. *Power and International Relations.* New York: Random House.

Claude, Inis. 1989. "The Balance of Power Revisited," *Review of International Studies* 15, 2: 77–85.

Cochran, Molly. 1999. *Normative Theory in International Relations: A Pragmatic Approach.* Cambridge: Cambridge University Press.

Cohn, Carol. 1987. "Sex and Death in the Rational World of Defense Intellectuals," *Signs* 12, 4: 687–718.

Cohn, Carol. 2006. "Motives and Methods: Using Multi-Sited Ethnography to Study US National Security Discourses," in Brooke Ackerly, Maria Stern, and Jacqui True (eds), *Feminist Methodologies for International Relations.* Cambridge, UK: Cambridge University Press: 91–107.

Cohn, Theodore H. 2012. *Global Political Economy,* 6th edn. Boston: Longman.

Confortini, Catia C. 2006. "Galtung, Violence, and Gender: The Case for a Peace Studies/ Feminism Alliance," *Peace & Change* 31, 3: 333–367.

Confortini, Catia C. 2012. *Intelligent Compassion:* Oxford: Oxford University Press.

Cox, Robert W., with Timothy J. Sinclair. 1996. *Approaches to World Order.* Cambridge: Cambridge University Press.

Cozette, Muriel. 2008. "What Lies Ahead: Classical Realism on the Future of International Relations," *International Studies Review* 10, 4: 667–679.

Crawford, Neta C. 2009. "Jürgen Habermas," in Jenny Edkins and Nick Vaughan-Williams (eds), *Critical Theorists and International Relations.* New York: Routledge: 187–198.

Critical Investigations into Humanitarianism in Africa. *The CIHA Blog.* www.cihablog.com.

Cutler, A. Claire. 1999. "Location 'Authority' in the Global Political Economy," *International Studies Quarterly* 43, 1: 59–81.

Cutler, A. Claire. 2002. "Critical Historical Materialism and International Law: Imagining International Law as Praxis," in Stephen Hobden and John M. Hobson (eds), *Historical Sociology of International Relations.* Cambridge: Cambridge University Press: 181–199.

Dalby, Simon. 1997. "Contesting an Essential Concept: Reading the Dilemmas in Contemporary Security Discourse," in Keith Krause & Michael C. Williams (eds), *Critical Security Studies.* Minneapolis: University of Minnesota Press, 3–31.

D'Costa, Bina. 2006. "Marginalized Identity: New Frontiers of Research for IR?" in Brooke A. Ackerly, Maria Stern, and Jacqui True (eds), *Feminist Methodologies for International Relations.* Cambridge: Cambridge University Press: 129–152.

Der Derian, James. 1987. *On Diplomacy.* Oxford: Basil Blackwell.

Der Derian, James, and Michael J. Shapiro. 1989. *International/Intertextual Relations: Postmodern Readings of World Politics.* Lanham, MD: Lexington Books.

Derrida, Jacques. 1976/1997. *Of Grammatology.* Baltimore, MD: Johns Hopkins University Press.

Dillon, Michael. 1996. *Politics of Security: Towards a Political Philosophy of Continental Thought.* New York: Routledge.

Doty, Roxanne Lynn. 1996. *Imperial Encounters: The Politics of Representation in North-South Relations.* Minneapolis: University of Minnesota Press.

Douven, Igor. 2011. "Abduction". *The Stanford Encyclopedia of Philosophy.* Edward N. Zalta (ed.) http://plato.stanford.edu/archives/spr2011/entries/abduction/. Accessed 5/6/2013.

Doyle, Michael. 1996. "Kant, Liberal Legacies, and Foreign Affairs," in Michael E. Brown, Sean M. Lynn-Jones, and Steven E. Miller (eds), *Debating the Democratic Peace.* Cambridge, MA: MIT Press: 3–57.

Dunn, Kevin. 2003. *Imagining the Congo: The International Relations of Identity.* New York: Palgrave Macmillan.

Dunne, Tim. 1998. *Inventing International Society: A History of the English School.* New York: St. Martin's Press.

Dunne, Tim, Milja Kurki, and Steve Smith. 2007. *International Relations Theories: Discipline and Diversity.* Oxford: Oxford University Press.

Duvall, Raymond, and Latha Varadarajan. 2007. "Traveling in Paradox: Edward Said and Critical International Relations," *Millennium: Journal of International Studies* 36, 1: 135–145.

Edkins, Jenny, and Nick Vaughan-Williams (eds). 2009. *Critical Theorists and International Relations.* New York: Routledge.

Elshtain, Jean Bethke. 1995. *Women and War.* Chicago: University of Chicago Press.

Enloe, Cynthia. 1989/2000. *Bananas, Beaches and Bases: Making Feminist Sense of International Politics.* Los Angeles: University of California Press.

Epstein, Charlotte. 2008. *The Power of Words in International Relations: Birth of an Anti-Whaling Discourse.* Cambridge, MA: MIT Press.

Esposito, John. 1999. *The Islamic Threat: Myth or Reality?* 3rd edn. New York: Oxford University Press.

Falk, Richard A. 1995. *On Humane Governance: Toward a New Global Project: The World Order Models Project Report of the Global Civilization Initiative.* University Park, PA: Pennsylvania State University Press.

Falk, Richard A., Mark Juergensmeyer, and Vesselin Popovski (eds). 2012. *Legality and Legitimacy in Global Affairs.* New York: Oxford University Press.

Fanon, Frantz. 1961/2005. *The Wretched of the Earth.* Richard Philcox (trans.) New York: Grove Press.

Fanon, Frantz. 1967. *Black Skin, White Masks.* Charles Lam Markmann (trans.) New York: Grove Weidenfeld.

Fierke, Karin M. 1998. *Changing Games, Changing Strategies: Critical Investigations in Security.* Manchester, UK: Manchester University Press.

Fierke, Karin M. 2001. "Critical Methodology and Constructivism," in Karin M. Fierke and Knud Eric Jørgensen (eds), *Constructing International Relations: The Next Generation.* Armonk, NY: M.E. Sharpe: 115–135.

Fierke, Karin M. 2009. "Agents of Death: The Structural Logic of Suicide Terrorism and Martyrdom," *International Theory* 1, 1: 155–184.

Fierke, Karin M., and Knud Eric Jørgensen. 2001. *Constructing International Relations: The Next Generation.* Armonk, NY: M.E. Sharpe.

Finnemore, Martha. 2004. *The Purpose of Intervention: Changing Beliefs about the Use of Force.* Ithaca, NY: Cornell University Press.

Foucault, Michel. 1977/1995. *Discipline & Punish: The Birth of the Prison,* 2nd edn. New York: Vintage Books.

Franklin, Peter. 2006/2012. "Dealing with Implicit Knowledge," 2012 post on blog, *Introducing Explication: Making the Implicit Explicit.* Abstracted from 2006 paper, "Explication as a Philosophical Enterprise," *Organizations and People* 13, 3: 6–11. Accessed 6/25/13.

Friedrichs, Jorge and Friedrich Kratochwil. 2009. "On Acting and Knowing: How Pragmatism Can Advance International Relations Research and Methodology," *International Organization* 63, 4: 701–31.

Frost, Mervyn. 1996. *Ethics in International Relations: A Constitutive Theory.* Cambridge: Cambridge University Press.

George, Jim. 1994. *Discourses of Global Politics: A Critical (Re)Introduction to International Relations.* Boulder, CO: Lynne Rienner.

Gill, Stephen (ed.) 1993. *Gramsci, Historical Materialism and International Relations.* Cambridge: Cambridge University Press.

Goff, Patricia M. 2007. *Limits to Liberalization: Local Culture in a Global Marketplace.* Ithaca, NY: Cornell University Press.

Gould, Harry D. 2010. *The Legacy of Punishment in International Law.* New York: Palgrave Macmillan.

Gramsci, Antonio. 1971/1999. *Selections from the Prison Notebooks.* New York: International Publishers.

Gramsci, Antonio. (Trans. and ed.) Derek Boothman. 1995. *Further Selections from the Prison Notebooks.* Minneapolis: University of Minnesota Press.

Grovogui, Siba N'Zatioula. 1996. *Sovereigns, Quasi-Sovereigns, and Africans.* Minneapolis: University of Minnesota Press.

Grovogui, Siba N'Zatioula. 2000. "Legal Standing, Questionable Deeds: Western Mediation in Namibia," in Cecelia Lynch and Michael Loriaux (eds), *Law and Moral Action in World Politics.* Minneapolis: University of Minnesota Press.

Grovogui, Siba N'Zatioula. 2006. *Beyond Eurocentrism and Anarchy.* New York: Palgrave Macmillan.

Guzzini, Stefano. 2005. "The Concept of Power: a Constructivist Analysis," *Millennium: Journal of International Studies* 33, 3: 495–521.

Habermas, Jürgen. 1990. "Moral Consciousness and Communicative Action," in *Moral Consciousness and Communicative Action.* Cambridge, MA: MIT Press: 116–194.

Habermas, Jürgen. 1996. *Between Facts and Norms: Contributions to a Discourse Theory of Law and Democracy.* Cambridge, MA: MIT Press.

Hansen, Lene. 2000. "The Little Mermaid's Silent Security Dilemma and the Absence of Gender in the Copenhagen School," *Millennium: Journal of International Studies* 29, 2: 285–306.

Hansen, Lene. 2006. *Security as Practice: Discourse Analysis and the Bosnian War.* New York: Routledge.

Haraway, Donna. [1988] 2003. *The Haraway Reader.* Psychology Press.

Harvey, David. 2005. *A Brief History of Neoliberalism.* Oxford, UK: Oxford University Press.

Hawkesworth, Mary. 2013. "Contending Conceptions of Science and Politics: Methodology and the Constitution of the Political," in Dvora Yanow and Peregrine Schwartz-Shea (eds), *Interpretation and Method: Empirical Research Methods and the Interpretive Turn.* Armonk, NY: M.E. Sharpe: 27–49.

Helleiner, Eric. 1994. *States and the Reemergence of Global Finance: From Bretton Woods to the 1990s.* Ithaca, NY: Cornell University Press.

Hesse, Mary. 1978. "Theory and Value in the Social Sciences," in C. Hookway and P. Pettit (eds), *Action and Interpretation: Studies in the Philosophy of the Social Sciences.* Cambridge: Cambridge University Press: 1–16.

Hollis, Martin, and Steve Smith. 1990. *Explaining and Understanding International Relations.* Oxford: Oxford University Press.

Hooper, Charlotte. 2001. *Manly States: Masculinities, International Relations, and Gender Politics.* New York: Columbia University Press.

Hosic, Aida. 2002. *Hollyworld: Space, Power and Fantasy in the American Economy.* Ithaca, NY: Cornell University Press.

Hunter, Shireen T. 1998. *The Future of Islam and the West: Clash of Civilizations or Peaceful Coexistence?* Westport: Praeger Publishers.

Huntington, Samuel. 1996. *The Clash of Civilizations and the Remaking of World Order.* New York: Touchstone.

Hutchings, Kimberly. 2010. *Global Ethics: An Introduction.* London: Polity Press.

Huysmans, Jeff. 2002. "Defining Social Constructivism in Security Studies: The Normative Dilemma of Writing Security" *Alternatives* 27, 1: 41–62.

Inayatullah, Naeem, and David L. Blaney. 2010. *Savage Economics: Wealth, Poverty and the Temporal Walls of Capitalism.* New York: Routledge.

Ishay, Micheline. 1995. *Internationalism and Its Betrayal.* Minneapolis: University of Minnesota Press.

Jackson, Patrick Thaddeus. 2011. *The Conduct of Inquiry in International Relations: Philosophy of Science and Its Implications for the Study of World Politics.* New York: Routledge.

Jackson, Peter. 2009. "Pierre Bourdieu," in Jenny Edkins and Nick Vaughan-Williams (eds), *Critical Theorists and International Relations.* New York: Routledge: 102–113.

Joll, James. 2000. *The Origins of the First World War*, 2nd edn. New York: Longman.

Juergensmeyer, Mark. 2008. *Global Rebellion: Religious Challenges to the Secular State*. Los Angeles: University of California Press.

Kennedy, David. 2000. "The International Style in Postwar Law and Policy," in Cecelia Lynch and Michael Loriaux (eds), *Law and Moral Action in World Politics*. Minneapolis: University of Minnesota Press: 54–76.

Keohane, Robert O., and Joseph S. Nye, Jr. 1977. *Power and Interdependence: World Politics in Transition*. Boston: Little, Brown and Co.

Kessler, Oliver, Rodney Bruce Hall, Cecelia Lynch, and Nicholas Onuf (eds). 2010. *On Rules, Politics and Knowledge: Friedrich Kratochwil, International Relations and Domestic Affairs*. New York: Palgrave Macmillan.

Kinnvall, Caterina. 2009. "Gayatri Chakravorty Spivak," in Jenny Edkins and Nick Vaughan-Williams (eds), *Critical Theorists and International Relations*. New York: Routledge: 317–329.

Kinsella, Helen. 2011. *The Image Before the Weapon: A Critical History of the Distinction between Combatant and Civilian*. Ithaca, NY: Cornell University Press.

Klotz, Audie, and Cecelia Lynch. 2007. *Strategies for Research in Constructivist International Relations*. Armonk, NY: M.E. Sharpe.

Klotz, Audie, and Deepa Prakash (eds). 2009. *Qualitative Methods in International Relations: A Pluralist Guide*. New York: Palgrave Macmillan.

Krasner, Stephen D. 1983. *International Regimes*. Ithaca, NY: Cornell University Press.

Kratochwil, Friedrich. 1989. *Rules, Norms and Decisions: On the Conditions of Practical and Legal Reasoning in International Relations and Domestic Affairs*. Cambridge: Cambridge University Press.

Kratochwil, Friedrich. 2011. *The Puzzles of Politics: Inquiries into the Genesis and Transformation of International Relations*. New York: Routledge.

Kratochwil, Friedrich, and John Gerard Ruggie. 1986. "International Organization: A State of the Art on an Art of the State," *International Organization* 40, 4: 753–775.

Krause, Keith, and Michael C. Williams. 1997. *Critical Security Studies*. Minneapolis: University of Minnesota Press.

Kubálková, Vendulka. 2000. "Towards and International Political Theology," *Millennium: Journal of International Studies* 29: 3: 675–704.

Kubálková, Vendulka (ed.) 2001. *Foreign Policy in a Constructed World*. Armonk, NY: M.E. Sharpe.

Kubálková, Vendulka, Nicholas Onuf, and Paul Kowert (eds). 1998. *International Relations in a Constructed World*. Armonk, NY: M.E. Sharpe.

Kurki, Milja. 2008. *Causation in International Relations: Reclaiming Causal Analysis*. Cambridge: Cambridge University Press.

Kurowska, Xymena, and Friedrich Kratochwil. 2012. "The Social Constructivist Sensibility and Research on Common Security and Defense Policy," in Xymena Kurowska and Fabian Breuer (eds), *Explaining the EU's Common Security and Defence Policy. Theory in Action*. New York: Palgrave: 86–110.

Kurowska, Xymena, and Benjamin Tallis. 2013. "Chiasmatic Crossings: A Reflexive Revisit of a Research Encounter in European Security," *Security Dialogue* 44, 1: 73–89.

Lamy, Steven, John Baylis, Steve Smith, and Patricia Owens. 2013. *Introduction to Global Politics*. Oxford: Oxford University Press.

Lang, Anthony F., Jr. 2008. *Punishment, Justice and International Relations: Ethics and Order After the Cold War*. London: Routledge.

Lapid, Yosef. 1989. "The Third Debate: On the Prospects of International Theory in a Post-Positivist Era," *International Studies Quarterly* 33, 3: 235–254.

Laudan, Larry. 1990. *Science and Relativism: Some Key Controversies in the Philosophy of Science.* Chicago: University of Chicago Press.

Lausten, Carsten Bagge, and Ole Wæver. 2000. "In Defence of Religion: Sacred Referent Objects for Securitization," *Millennium: Journal of International Studies* 29, 3: 705–739.

Leander, Anna. 2008. "Thinking Tools," in Audie Klotz and Deepa Prakash (eds). *Qualitative Methods in International Relations.* New York: Palgrave Macmillan: 11–27.

Lebow, Richard Ned. 2003. *The Tragic Vision of Politics: Ethics, Interests, and Orders.* Cambridge, UK: Cambridge University Press.

Lebow, Richard Ned. 2007. "Classical Realism," in *International Relations Theories. Discipline and Diversity.* Oxford: Oxford University Press, 52–70.

Leebaw, Bronwyn. 2011. *Judging State-Sponsored Violence: Imagining Political Change.* Cambridge: Cambridge University Press.

Ling, Lily H.M. 2002. *Postcolonial International Relations: Conquest and Desire Between Asia and the West.* New York: Palgrave Macmillan.

Lipschutz, Ronnie, and Ken Conca (eds). 1993. *The State and Social Power in Global Environmental Politics.* New York: Columbia University Press.

Litfin, Karen T. 1994. *Ozone Discourse.* New York: Columbia University Press.

Long, David, and Brian C. Schmidt (eds). 2005. *Imperialism and Internationalism in the Discipline of International Relations.* Albany: State University of New York Press.

Long, David, and Peter Wilson (eds). 1995. *Thinkers of the Twenty-Years' Crisis: Interwar Idealism Reassessed.* Oxford, UK: Oxford University Press.

Loriaux, Michael. 1992. "The Realists and Saint Augustine: Skepticism, Psychology, and Moral Action in International Relations Thought," *International Studies Quarterly* 36: 401–420.

Loriaux, Michael. 2000. "Law and Moral Action in International Relations Thought," in Cecelia Lynch and Michael Loriaux (eds), *Law and Moral Action in World Politics.* Minneapolis: University of Minnesota Press: xi–xxiii.

Loriaux, Michael. 2008. *European Union and the Deconstruction of the Rhineland Frontier.* Cambridge: Cambridge University Press.

Lu, Catherine. 2006. *Just and Unjust Interventions in World Politics.* New York: Palgrave Macmillan.

Luke, Timothy W. 1997. *Ecocritique.* Minneapolis: University of Minnesota Press.

Lynch, Cecelia. 1994. "Kant, the Republican Peace, and Moral Guidance in International Law," *Ethics & International Affairs* 8, 1: 39–58.

Lynch, Cecelia. 1998. "Social Movements and the Problem of Globalization". *Alternatives* 23: 149–173.

Lynch, Cecelia. 1999. *Beyond Appeasement: Interpreting Interwar Peace Movements in World Politics.* Ithaca, NY: Cornell University Press.

Lynch, Cecelia. 2000. "Dogma, Praxis, and Religious Perspectives on Multiculturalism," *Millennium: Journal of International Studies* 29, 3: 741–759.

Lynch, Cecelia. 2009. "A Neo-Weberian Approach to Religion in International Politics," *International Theory* 1, 3: 381–408.

Lynch, Cecelia. 2010. "Debating Moral Agency and International Law in an NGO World," in Oliver Kessler, Rodney Bruce Hall, Cecelia Lynch, and Nicholas Onuf (eds), *On Rules, Politics and Knowledge: Friedrich Kratochwil and the Study of International Relations.* New York: Palgrave Macmillan: 145–157.

Lynch, Cecelia. 2011. "Religious Humanitarianism and the Global Politics of Secularism," in Craig Calhoun, Mark Juergensmeyer, and Jonathan VanAntwerpen (eds), *Rethinking Secularism*. Oxford: Oxford University Press: 204–224.

Lynch, Cecelia and Michael Loriaux (eds). 2000. *Law and Moral Action in World Politics*. Minneapolis: University of Minnesota Press.

Marx, Karl. 1845. "Theses on Feuerbach," in *Marx and Engels Internet Archive*. Marxists Internet Archive (MIA): www.marxists.org/index.htm, accessed 8/13.

Mbembe, Achille. 2001. *On the Postcolony*. Berkeley and Los Angeles: University of California Press.

Milliken, Jennifer. 1999. "The Study of Discourse in International Relations: A Critique of Research and Methods," *European Journal of International Relations* 5, 2: 225–254.

Mitzen, Jennifer. 2006. "Ontological Security in World Politics: State Identity and the Security Dilemma," *European Journal of International Relations* 12, 3: 341–370.

Morgenthau, Hans J. 1946. *Scientific Man vs. Power Politics*. Chicago: University of Chicago Press.

Morgenthau, Hans J. 1978. *Politics Among Nations*, 5th edn. New York: Alfred Knopf.

Muppidi, Himadeep. 1999. "Postcoloniality and the Production of International Insecurity: The Persistent Puzzle of U.S.-Indian Relations," in Jutta Weldes, Mark Laffey, Hugh Gusterson and Raymond Duvall (eds), *Cultures of Insecurity: States, Communities, and the Production of Danger*. Minneapolis: University of Minnesota Press, 119–146.

Muppidi, Himadeep. 2009. "Frantz Fanon," in Jenny Edkins and Nick Vaughan-Williams (eds), *Critical Theorists and International Relations*. New York: Routledge: 150–160.

Murphy, Craig. 1994. *International Organization and Industrial Change: Global Governance since 1850*. Oxford: Polity Press and Oxford University Press.

Nardin, Terry. 1983. *Law, Morality, and the Relations of States*. Princeton: Princeton University Press.

Neumann, Iver B. 2012. *At Home with the Diplomats: Inside a European Foreign Ministry*. Ithaca, NY: Cornell University Press.

Nexon, Daniel H. 2009. *The Struggle for Power in Early Modern Europe*. Princeton: Princeton University Press.

Niebuhr, Reinhold. 1932/2002. *Moral Man and Immoral Society: A Study in Ethics and Politics*. Louisville, KY: Westminster John Knox Press.

Onuf, Nicholas. 1989. *World of Our Making*. Columbia, SC: University of South Carolina Press.

Onuf, Nicholas. 1998. *The Republican Legacy in International Thought*. Cambridge: Cambridge University Press.

Onuf, Nicholas. 2002. "'Tainted by Contingency': Retelling the Story of International Law," in Richard Falk, Lester Ruiz, and R.B.J. Walker (eds), *Reframing the International: Law, Culture, Politics*. New York: Routledge, 26–45.

Onuf, Nicholas. 2012. *Making Sense, Making Worlds*. New York: Routledge.

Oren, Ido. 2003. *Our Enemies & US: America's Rivalries and the Making of Political Science*. Ithaca, NY: Cornell University Press.

Oxford English Dictionary. 1993. "Abduction". Oxford: Clarendon Press: 888.

Palan, Rolan. 2003. "Susan Strange's Vision for a Critical International Political Economy," in Harry Bauer and Elisabetta Brighi (eds), *International Relations at LSE; A History of 75 Years*. London: Millennium Publishing Group.

Peoples, Columba, and Nick Vaughan-Williams. 2010. *Critical Security Studies: An Introduction*. New York: Routledge.

Persaud, Randolph B., and R.B.J. Walker (eds). 2001. "Race in International Relations," Special Issue of *Alternatives* 26, 4.

Peterson, V. Spike. 2003. *A Critical Rewriting of Global Political Economy.* New York: Routledge.

Peterson, V. Spike, and Anne Sisson Runyan. 1999. *Global Gender Issues,* 2nd edn.

Petito, Fabio, and Pavlos Hatzopoulos. 2003. *Religion in International Relations: The Return from Exile.* New York: Palgrave Macmillan.

Pettman, Jan Jindy. 1996. *Worlding Women: A Feminist International Politics.* New York: Routledge.

Philpott, Daniel. 2000. *Revolutions in Sovereignty: The Religious Roots of Modern International Relations.* Princeton: Princeton University Press.

Polanyi, Karl. 1944/1957. *The Great Transformation: The Political and Economic Origins of Our Time.* Boston: Beacon Press.

Prügl, Elisabeth. 1998. "Feminist Struggle as Social Construction: Changing the Gendered Rules of Home-Based Work," in Vendulka Kubálková, Nicholas Onuf, and Paul Kowert (eds), *International Relations in a Constructed World.* Armonk, NY: M.E. Sharpe: 123–146.

Prügl, Elisabeth. 1999. *The Global Construction of Gender: Home-Based Work in the Political Economy of the 20th Century.* New York: Columbia University Press.

Rabinow, Paul (ed.) 1984. *The Foucault Reader.* London: Penguin Books.

Ramberg, Bjørn and Gjesdal, Kristin, "Hermeneutics," *The Stanford Encyclopedia of Philosophy* (Summer 2009 edition), Edward N. Zalta (ed.), http://plato.stanford.edu/archives/sum2009/entries/hermeneutics/, accessed 4.27.12.

Rengger, Nicholas. 1995. *Political Theory, Modernity, and Postmodernity: Beyond Enlightenment and Critique.* Oxford: Basil Blackwell.

Reus-Smit, Christian. 1999. *The Moral Purpose of the State.* Princeton: Princeton University Press.

Roach, Steven C. 2008. *Critical Theory and International Relations: A Reader.* New York: Routledge.

Robinson, Fiona. 2011. *The Ethics of Care: A Feminist Approach to Human Security.* Philadelphia: Temple University Press.

Rorty, Richard. 2004. "A Pragmatist View of Contemporary Analytic Philosophy," in William Egginton and Mike Sandbothe (eds), *The Pragmatic Turn in Philosophy: Contemporary Engagements between Analytic and Continental Thought.* SUNY-Binghamton: SUNY Press: 131–144.

Rosenberg, Justin. 1990. *The Empire of Civil Society.* London: Verso Press.

Ruggie, John Gerard. 1982. "International Regimes, Transactions, and Change: Embedded Liberalism in the Postwar Economic Order," *International Organization* 36, 2: 379–415.

Ruggie, John Gerard. 1998. *Constructing the World Polity: Essays on International Institutionalization.* New York: Routledge.

Said, Edward. 1979. *Orientalism.* New York: Vintage Press.

Scheurmann, William. 2010. "The (Classical) Realist Vision of Global Reform," *International Theory* 2, 2: 246–282.

Schwartz-Shea, Peregrine, and Dvora Yanow. 2012. *Interpretive Research Design: Concepts and Processes.* New York: Routledge.

Sen, Gita, and Caren Grown. 1998. *Development Crises and Alternative Visions.* New York: Routledge.

Sending, Ole Jacob, and Iver Neumann. 2006. "Governance to Governmentality: Analyzing NGOs, States, and Power," *International Studies Quarterly* 50: 651–672.

Shakman Hurd, Elizabeth. 2008. *The Politics of Secularism in International Relations.* Princeton: Princeton University Press.

Shaw, Timothy M., and Lucian M. Ashworth. 2010. "Commonwealth Perspectives on International Relations," *International Affairs* 86, 5: 1149–1165.

Sheikh, Mona. 2011. "Guardians of God: Understanding the Religious Violence of Pakistan's Taliban." Ph.D. Dissertation, University of Copenhagen.

Shepherd, Laura (ed.) 2010. *Gender Matters in Global Politics: A Feminist Introduction to International Relations.* New York: Routledge.

Shepherd, Laura. 2012. *Gender, Violence, and Popular Culture: Telling Stories.* New York: Routledge.

Shou Talve, Vibeke. 2008. *Realist Strategies of Republican Peace: Morgenthau, Niebuhr, and the Politics of Patriotism as Dissent.* New York: Palgrave Macmillan.

Shusterman, Richard (ed.) 1999. *Bourdieu, A Critical Reader.* Oxford: Blackwell.

Sil, Rudra, and Peter J. Katzenstein. 2010. *Analytic Eclecticism in the Study of World Politics.* New York: Palgrave Macmillan.

Smith, Michael J. 1987. *Realist Thought from Weber to Kissinger.* Baton Rouge: Louisiana State University Press.

Spivak, Gayatri Chakravorty. 1988. "Can the Subaltern Speak?," in Cary Nelson and Lawrence Grossberg (eds), *Marxism and the Interpretation of Culture.* Urbana: University of Illinois Press: 271–313.

Spivak, Gayatri Chakravorty. 1998. *In Other Worlds: Essays in Cultural Politics.* New York: Routledge.

Srinha, Mrinalini. 1995. *Colonial Masculinity: The "Manly Englishman" and the "Effeminate Bengali" in the Late Nineteenth Century.* Manchester: Manchester University Press.

Steele, Brent J. 2008. *Ontological Security in International Relation: Self-Identity and the IR State.* New York: Routledge.

Stern, Maria. 2006. "Racism, Sexism, Classism, and Much More: Reading Security-Identity in Marginalized Sites," in Brooke A. Ackerly, Maria Stern, and Jacqui True (eds), *Feminist Methodologies for International Relations.* Cambridge: Cambridge University Press: 174–198.

Strange, Susan. 1986. *Casino Capitalism.* Oxford: Basil Blackwell.

Strange, Susan. 1987. *States and Markets.* London: Pinter.

Strange, Susan. 1996. *The Retreat of the State: The Diffusion of Power in the World Economy.* Cambridge: Cambridge University Press.

Struett, Michael J. 2008. *The Politics of Constructing the International Criminal Court: NGOs, Discourse, and Agency.* New York: Palgrave Macmillan.

Sylvester, Christine. 1994. *Feminist Theory and International Relations in a Postmodern Era.* Cambridge: Cambridge University Press.

Sylvester, Christine. 2007. "Anatomy of a Footnote," *Security Dialogue* 38, 4: 547–558.

Taylor, Charles. 1971. "Interpretation and the Sciences of Man," *Review of Metaphysics* 25, 1: 3–51; reprinted in Fred Dallmayr and Thomas A. McCarthy (eds). 1977. *Understanding and Social Inquiry.* Notre Dame, IN: University of Notre Dame Press.

Taylor, Charles. 2007. *A Secular Age.* Cambridge, MA: Harvard University Press.

Thomas, Scott M. 2000. "Taking Religious and Cultural Pluralism Seriously: The Global Resurgence of Religion and the Transformation of International Society," *Millennium: Journal of International Studies* 29, 3: 815–841.

Thomas, Scott M. 2005. *The Global Resurgence of Religion and the Transformation of International Relations.* New York: Palgrave Macmillan.

Tickner, Arlene B. 2008. "Latin American IR and the Primacy of *lo practico*," *International Studies Review* 10, 4: 735–748.

Tickner, Arlene B., and Ole Wæver (eds). 2009. *International Relations Scholarship Around the World*. New York: Routledge.

Tickner, J. Ann. 1988. "Hans Morgenthau's Principles of Political Realism: A Feminist Reformulation," *Millennium: Journal of International Studies* 17, 3: 429–440.

Tickner, J. Ann. 1992. *Gender in International Relations: Feminist Perspectives on Achieving Global Security*. New York: Columbia University Press.

Tickner, J. Ann. 1997. "You Just Don't Understand: Troubled Engagements Between Feminists and IR Theorists," *International Studies Quarterly* 41, 4: 611–632.

Tickner, J. Ann, and Laura Sjoberg. 2007. "Feminism," in Tim Dunne, Milja Kurki, and Steve Smith (eds), *International Relations Theories: Discipline and Diversity*. Oxford: Oxford University Press: 185–202.

Tronto, Joan. 1993. *Moral Boundaries: A Political Argument for an Ethic of Care*. New York: Routledge.

True, Jacqui. 2003. *Gender, Globalization, and Postsocialism: The Czech Republic After Communism*. New York: Columbia University Press.

True, Jacqui. 2012. *The Political Economy of Violence Against Women*. New York: Oxford University Press.

Turner, Stephen and Ido Oren. 2009. "Hans J. Morgenthau and the Legacy of Max Weber," in Duncan Bell (ed.), *Political Thought and International Relations: Variations on a Realist Theme*. Oxford: Oxford University Press: 63–82.

Vitalis, Robert. 2010. "The Noble American Science of Imperial Relations and Its Laws of Race Development," *Comparative Studies of Society and History* 52, 4: 909–938.

Walker, R.B.J. 1990. "Security, Sovereignty and the Challenge of World Politics," *Alternatives* 1: 3–27.

Walker, R.B.J. 1993. *Inside/Outside: International Relations as Political Theory*. Cambridge: University of Cambridge Press.

Walker, R.B.J. 2010. *After the Globe: Before the World*. New York: Routledge.

Waltz, Kenneth. 1979. *Theory of International Politics*. Addison-Wesley.

Wæver, Ole. 1995. "Securitization and Desecuritization," in Ronnie Lipschutz (ed.), *On Security*. New York: Columbia University Press: 46–86.

Weber, Cynthia. 2005. *International Relations Theory: A Critical Introduction*. New York: Routledge.

Weber, Max. 2011. *Methodology of Social Sciences*. New Jersey: Transaction Publishers.

Weldes, Jutta. 1999. "The Cultural Production of Crises: U.S. Identity and Missiles in Cuba," in Jutta Weldes, Mark Laffey, Hugh Gusterson, and Raymond Duvall (eds), *Cultures of Insecurity: States, Communities, and the Production of Danger*. Minneapolis: University of Minnesota Press, 35–62.

Weldes, Jutta. 2013. "High Politics and Low Data: Globalization Discourses and Popular Culture," in Dvora Yanow and Peregrine Schwartz-Shea (eds), *Interpretation and Method: Empirical Research Methods and the Interpretive Turn*. Armonk, NY: M.E. Sharpe: 228–238.

Weldes, Jutta, Mark Laffey, Hugh Gusterson, and Raymond Duvall. 1999. *Cultures of Insecurity: States, Communities, and the Production of Danger*. Minneapolis: University of Minnesota Press.

Wendt, Alexander. 1987. "The Agent-Structure Problem in International Relations Theory," *International Organization* 41, 3: 335–370.

Wendt, Alexander. 1992. "Anarchy is What States Make of It: The Social Construction of Power Politics," *International Organization* 46, 2: 391–425.

Whitworth, Sandra. 1994. *Feminism and International Relations: Towards a Political Economy of Gender in Multilateral Institutions.* New York: Macmillan Press.

Wibben, Annick T.R. 2011. *Feminist Security Studies: A Narrative Approach.* London: Routledge.

Wight, Martin. 2002. *Power Politics.* London: Continuum Press.

Williams, Michael C. 2004. "Why Ideas Matter in International Relations: Hans Morgenthau, Classical Realism, and the Moral Construction of Power Politics," *International Organization* 58: 633–665.

Williams, Michael C. 2005. *The Realist Tradition and the Limits of International Relations.* Cambridge: Cambridge University Press.

Williams, Michael C., and Keith Krause (eds). 1997. *Critical Security Studies: Concepts and Strategies.* New York: Routledge.

Wilson, Erin. 2011. *After Secularism: Rethinking Religion in Global Politics.* New York: Palgrave Macmillan.

Wittgenstein, Ludwig. 1953/1958. *Philosophical Investigations,* 2nd edn. Oxford: Blackwell.

Wolfers, Arnold. 1952. "'National Security' as an Ambiguous Symbol," *Political Science Quarterly* 67, 4: 481–502.

Yanow, Dvora, and Peregrine Schwartz-Shea (eds). 2013. *Interpretation and Method: Empirical Research Methods and the Interpretive Turn.* Armonk, NY: M.E. Sharpe.

Young, Oran. 1983. "Regime Dynamics: The Rise and Fall of International Regimes," in Stephen D. Krasner (ed.), *International Regimes.* Ithaca, NY: Cornell University Press, 93–115.

Zehfuss, Maja, and Jenny Edkins (eds). 2009. *Global Politics: A New Introduction.* London: Routledge.

INDEX